Reconciliation and Liberation

Challenging a One-Dimensional View of Salvation

Jan Milič Lochman

Translated by David Lewis

FORTRESS PRESS   PHILADELPHIA

Translated from the German *Versöhnung und Befreiung*, copyright ©
1977 by Gütersloher Verlagshaus Gerd Mohn, Gütersloh, Germany.

Scripture quotations:
From *The New English Bible*. © The Delegates of the Oxford Universi-
ty Press and The Syndics of the Cambridge University Press 1961, 1970.
Reprinted by permission.
From the Today's English Version of the New Testament. Copyright ©
American Bible Society 1966.

Quotations on pages 126-27 and 136-37 are reprinted with permission
of Macmillan Publishing Co., Inc. and SCM Press Ltd. from *Letters
and Papers from Prison,* The Enlarged Edition, by Dietrich Bonhoeffer.
Copyright © 1953, 1967, 1971 by SCM Press, Ltd.

English edition copyright © 1980 by Christian Journals Ltd.

First English Edition by Christian Journals Ltd., 1980
First American Edition by Fortress Press, 1980

Library of Congress Cataloging in Publication Data

Lochman, Jan Milič.
  Reconciliation and liberation.

  Translation of Versöhnung und Befreiung.
  1. Salvation. I. Title.
BT751.2.L6213   1980   234   78-54555
ISBN 0-8006-1340-6

7405D80   Printed in the United States of America   1-1340

Contents

Prefatory Note: The translation of the Bible generally used in this work is the *New English Bible.* Occasionally the translator has turned to another version where this accorded more with the German version used by the author. Wherever possible, existing translations of works cited by the author have been used, always with care.

The author's mother tongue is Czech and his German could be described as an 'inter-language' with an expressive flavour all its own. Preferring 'dynamic fidelity' to flamboyant infidelity, the translator has kept fairly closely to the author's text and the version presented here has the author's approval. There are times, as T. S. Eliot once pointed out, when it is the 'spirit' that kills and the 'letter' that giveth life.

Introduction

My purpose in writing this book is to develop a comprehensive ecumenical view of salvation. This is a never-ending task, since the relationship between God and humanity, heaven and earth, salvation history and world history, is an inseparable part of the very core and pattern of the biblical faith, luminously so in the story of Jesus Christ. The theme of theology is two-dimensional in virtue of its biblical basis. If we adopt the ecumenical jargon and speak of a 'vertical' dimension and a 'horizontal' dimension, we shall have to say that these two dimensions intersect, symbolically and in reality, in the cross of Jesus, in the apostolic 'Gospel of the cross'. These two dimensions are neither confused nor separated, but constitute an indissoluble unity. Only so do they provide the total theme of theology.

But in the Church and in the world, people very often lose patience with the tension between the two dimensions. They consider it intolerable and even absurd. They try in one way or another to soften it and even to eliminate it altogether. Some regard Christianity as a purely redemptive religion requiring the radical renunciation of this world and promising eternal bliss in the life to come. They then either accept it as a haven of pure spirituality or else reject it as the 'opium of the people'. Others seek to play down and excise from the biblical message the longing for God, this 'Wholly Other' who 'changes everything',[1] regarding it as a purely contingent cultural accessory. This clears the decks for an undistracted effort to get to the heart of the matter and to press forward with the really important task, that of 'changing' the world.

The strategy in both cases is the same: the *dialogical alliance* between the two dimensions is replaced by a *monological rivalry*. A one-dimensional view of salvation is adopted. The two beams of the one cross are wrenched apart.

My personal experience as a theologian and churchman in both East and West has taught me how questionable and dangerous such one-dimensional views of salvation are, for the reason just given and also in view of the actual situation of the Church today. In three very different contexts — in a Marxist socialist society, in a liberal capitalist society, and in the life of the ecumenical movement — serious damage is done to the authenticity and integrity of the Church's witness and service when it is mistakenly supposed that we have to choose between either 'verticalists' or 'horizontalists'. The result is a tendency for our church life to polarize into opposing sectarian groups all flourishing their rival banners and defending their cherished life-styles. Accusations are bandied about, one side accusing the other of 'pietistic escapism' and being accused in turn of 'politicization' or 'escape into politics'. Parties are formed in ecumenical circles, in synods, even in local congregations, and outbid one another in the struggle for theological influence and political clout. Resources urgently needed for more constructive tasks are thereby squandered.

It may help us to move forward from entrenched positions into genuine dialogue, if we look again at the biblical basis and contemporary contexts of the message of salvation, and try to develop an unpretentious 'doctrine of salvation' for pastors and lay people. Although the term 'salvation' is somewhat tainted for many people today, especially in German-speaking countries, it has one advantage, I believe, over the term 'redemption'. It is already impregnated with the biblical history of salvation and is therefore inherently comprehensive, very much in the same way as the biblical term for peace (*shalom*). It has a built-in defence against attempts to compartmentalize faith and make it one-dimensional, whether by sacralizing it completely or secularizing it completely. Certainly salvation in the biblical sense must be understood, received and practiced both as reconciliation *and* liberation. In other words, holistically, comprehensively. My main purpose in this book is to offer a modest contribution to the promotion of this truth. Both my personal experiences and the heritage of the Czech Reformation in which I stand also help to explain my concern with this theme.

Basel.

Jan Milič Lochman

1

An Ecumenical 'Geometry' of Salvation

Salvation machines

An efficient land is this
Of clean and tidy people
And salvation machines
Operating with painful precision.

On the assembly line
Each citizen at birth
Is placed, still kicking,
For automatic, ceremonious
Drilling, until finally
The last rites lovingly
Deliver her or him
Into Elysian fields.

An efficient land is this
Of clean and tidy people
And salvation machines
Operating with painful precision.

Kurt Marti

These lines of a Swiss pastor and poet, Kurt Marti, make a good starting point for our reflections on the theology of salvation. Provoking and cryptic, Marti's poem illuminated the background of experience against which the question of salvation arises (and is distorted) for many of us today, if it occurs to us at all. As with all good poems, this one, too, makes sense in a variety of contexts. Pastors will at once be reminded of the ambiguities of life in an *established Church*. Marti may well have been thinking of his own Canton of Berne, but it applies to other Swiss Cantons, indeed, to other countries like Germany and England, for example. In this 'efficient land' of 'clean and tidy people', anyone born here is taken, as soon after birth as possible ('still kicking'), more or less 'lovingly' in hand, with the promise and claim of baptism and other rites which form part of the Church's machinery of salvation, and then, more or less efficiently, processed throughout life — by religious instruction, confirmation, marriage, the baptism of children and grandchildren, then perhaps a long period interrupted only by an occasional visit to church for a special service or fast-day sermon, until 'finally' he or she, or more often than not simply 'it', is delivered 'into Elysian fields', perhaps via the crematorium, decked with wreaths and cossetted with ceremonies.

I am caricaturing, of course. With a modicum of goodwill, other more positive features could be pointed out and even the ones I have mentioned presented in a more favourable light. Yet for all its over-simplification, the caricature highlights the fact that for most of its members, mostly inactive members, the established Church operates as a 'salvation machine'.

We could turn the spotlight of this poem on other contexts, too, of course. It makes us think, not only of the ecclesiastical 'assembly line' but of the social 'assembly lines', too, of the secular 'salvation machines' which 'operate with painful precision'. We are reminded of an obvious and menacing feature of contemporary society: the tendency of modern economic and political systems to control citizens as completely as possible. This tendency is not confined to any particular social system, though it takes different forms in different systems. It is particularly noticeable in Eastern socialist systems, of course, where a constant effort is made to bring citizens and all aspects of their lives under a centralized ideological and political surveillance and control. But the same tendency is also observable in the capitalist societies of the West, even if more scope is allowed here for diversity and plurality. Here we find a competitive 'market economy' which nevertheless also tends by its very nature to impose the desired patterns of behaviour on the citizens, whether as consumers or as units of a dependent labour force, whether by gentle persuasion or by more explicit economic pressures.

These methods of surveillance, control and manipulation are extended and refined in both East and West by the achievements of modern science and technology, in a degree hardly parallelled in previous history. They invade every aspect of public and even private life. In the age of the computer and data-processing, technological advances draw the meshes tighter and tighter. The machines operate with 'painful precision'.

Of special interest to us in relation to the theme of this book is the third point to which Marti's poem draws attention, namely, the question of *salvation*. The 'assembly lines' do not appear as 'naked aggressors' or as the sheer pressures of economic and political systems. They present themselves not as

11

machinery for domination and alienation, but as desirable 'salvation machines', decked out and transfigured ceremoniously. In the East, the Party claims that by its ideological regimentation it is protecting the real interests of its citizens in the most far-sighted way possible. Indeed, it is scientifically preparing the parousia of the 'new humanity' which is the ultimate goal of history. In the West, the claim is made that here is the 'Free World', or at least the world which provides the maximum possible 'private' happiness. An analysis of the 'soteriologies' (i.e. doctrines of salvation) which underlie ideological propaganda and the advertizing industry from this standpoint would be most instructive.

At least two points of importance for our theme arise from this third emphasis in Marti's poem. Firstly, *salvation themes continue to appear* in modern culture, modern economies and modern societies. The complaint is sometimes heard in theological and church circles that our secularized contemporaries are losing all interest in salvation. If it refers to the traditional form of the question of salvation and its conscious articulation, the complaint is well-founded. But the disappearance of the traditional form of the question does not mean that the problem of redemption itself has sunk without trace. It has simply shifted its ground. In any study of the doctrine of salvation this phenomenon needs to be looked at very critically. Not simply to make theological capital out of the situation, of course. Not with any idea of warming up our own lukewarm religious or theological soup on the still smouldering fire of secular hopes of salvation. But certainly in order to enter into a dialogue with these secular hopes. To do this, moreover, not simply in order to size them up for

12

refutation but also with a view to critically reexamining our own traditional doctrines of salvation. Questions to be asked would include the following: Has not this traditional soteriology been onesided in its emphases when interpreting the hope of salvation? Has it not thereby aroused hopes of salvation of a very different kind? In what follows we shall, of course, have some very critical questions of our own to put to the modern 'salvation machines', but we shall try not to lose sight of the critical questions to be addressed to ourselves.

The second point arising from this third emphasis in Marti's poem is a *material* one concerning the critical problems arising from its protest against a *mechanical* and *one-dimensional view of salvation*. Both these adjectives must be taken seriously. They pinpoint two basic tendencies in the contemporary misconception of salvation. First, the mechanical aspect. In the preparatory booklet for the Bangkok Missionary Conference on 'Salvation Today' in which Marti's poem appeared, the Swiss theologian Klauspeter Blaser commented: 'Marti in his poem succeeds in capturing a very real element in the alienation of salvation. He might well have entitled his poem "Salvation comes from the machine", because the machines stand for a world which is geared to productive efficiency'.[2] The poem undoubtedly envisages the technocratic alienation of salvation, the 'painful precision' of the systems and mechanisms which 'protect' human beings. We must remember, however, that the poem is referring not just to the technological and economic machines but also, and above all, to the theological and ecclesiastical machines. As Blaser correctly notes, the rallying cry offered to us in the Bible is not 'Salvation comes from the machines' but 'Salvation comes from the Jews', which is quite a different

13

thing. A very different view of salvation is implied in this biblical slogan. Blaser explains it in the following polemical words: 'Salvation is found neither *in* a system nor *as* a system but only wherever real life, freedom and happiness shatter the salvation systems and the planned and the predictable can expect to be disturbed. Resurrection? Judgement? Grace? Might it not then actually be true that salvation comes from the Jews?'.[3]

These incisive questions, particularly the reference to resurrection, judgement and grace (the basic data of the biblical history of salvation), brings us to the second aspect of the alienation of salvation in the life of society and the Church, namely, the *one-dimensional* view of salvation. All salvation systems and machines have this tendency. A one-dimensional view of salvation enables them to operate more smoothly, 'interference free', with 'painful' (or agreeable) 'precision'. Unidimensional man is far easier to direct and control. Herbert Marcuse's analysis of human alienation along these lines is therefore to be taken very seriously. It fits all salvation machines, both eastern style and western. Take for example the repeated, almost desperate efforts of Stalinist and neo-Stalinist hard-liners to whip up new anti-God crusades despite the fact that such campaigns are almost invariably a failure. May the explanation not be that faith in God, the message of judgement and resurrection, are a challenge to one-dimensionality? They constitute a random factor in a system which claims officially to exercise a political and cultural monopoly. This profound ideological and party-political vested interest demands their exclusion, therefore, as far as possible. For the party officials the essential thing is that the 'salvation machine' should run smoothly. It is this vested interest — dogmatic rather than

14

Marxist, mechanistic rather than based on historical materialism — which makes atheism something devoutly to be wished.

The pressure towards a corresponding one-dimensionality is not as clearly defined or as ideologically rigid among the western technocrats, the barons of industry and culture. The same tendencies nevertheless exist, but they take a different form. They also have their materialistic and their open or concealed atheistic features. Here, too, the human being is to be 'explained' and manipulated as an object — if possible completely, and therefore as one-dimensionally as possible. Critical questions need to be addressed on this score to technologically-minded sociologists and psychologists, to certain secular and religious therapists and, of course, to the strategists and ideologues of the mass media and the advertizing industry. The deliberate or at least *de facto* elimination of theological issues in these areas is not necessarily proof of a realistic secular approach but more often of a dogmatic secularistic one, interested primarily in the smooth operation of its own 'salvation machine'.

But the tendency to a one-dimensional view of salvation in our western culture and in our churches takes another form, too. Here an attempt is made to exclude any possible 'interference factor' (faith, God, judgement, resurrection) not by directly denying it but by limiting its scope. The idea is to corral and channel it into religious ghettos and reservations. Using the geometrical jargon of the notorious theological controversies of recent years, there is not only a 'horizontal' but also a 'vertical' one-dimensional view of salvation. 'Horizontalism' means, of course, the equation of salvation with the solution of historical social problems. Some Orthodox and evangelical groups suspect or accuse the ecumenical movement of having done this in the years from Uppsala to Nairobi. 'Verticalism', on the other hand, means the tendency to see salvation in strictly metaphysical and individualistic terms; to restrict questions about God, grace, judgement and resurrection to the purely private and personal realm. But this is also to be one-dimensional, and in just as questionable a way. Here, too, the interference or nuisance factor is neutralized and domesticated.

The Church and religion are not persecuted, of course. They are not even challenged. So long as believers leave the other dimension — the 'horizontal' dimension of economics, politics and culture — to the competent authorities and powers, they are perfectly at liberty to live their religious lives in private and even to make use of the Church's ministrations as 'private account' customers. Clearly this 'vertical' version of the one-dimensional approach to salvation is the one adopted and fostered in many circles, especially conservative ones. There is no mistaking the alarm they feel when other Christians — in the ecumenical movement, for example, or in committed action groups within or on the fringe of our established churches — venture into the social field with their message of salvation!

It is not so easy — least of all for faithful church members — to recognize and admit that this 'vertical' one-dimensional approach also distorts and alienates the Gospel of salvation. Theologians and even the Church itself have all too frequently encouraged this misunderstanding by a lopsided and sometimes exclusive emphasis on the 'vertical' dimension of salvation in their presentation of the Gospel. Let me give one or two examples.

In the article on 'salvation' (*soteria*) in Kittel's well-known *Theological Dictionary of the New*

Testament, we find the following categorical statement: 'NT *soteria* does not refer to earthly conditions. Its content is not, as in the Greek understanding, well-being, health of body and soul. Nor is it the earthly liberation of the people of God from the heathen yoke, as in Judaism. It does not relate to any circumstances as such. It denotes neither healing in the religious sense, nor life, nor liberation from satanic or demonic power. It has to do solely with man's relationship to God'.[4]

Faced with such an unbalanced and narrow interpretation of the concept of salvation, one can only register astonishment that a reputable New Testament scholar could lend his authority to it.

But even the systematic theologians have lent their support to an equally verticalist distortion of the idea of salvation. One example will suffice: the whole thrust of the 'two kingdoms doctrine' which has been so influential in the history of the Church. In the extreme versions of this doctrine, the concept of salvation was strictly insulated from secular questions. In consequence, whole areas of human life were put out of reach of salvation so that these areas were, so to speak, immunized against soteriology and ethics. This narrow, reductionist view of salvation owes more to idealist and dualist ways of thinking than to the Bible. It is no more satisfactory as a 'geometry of salvation' than its opposite extreme, the horizontalist and secularist view of salvation. Here again let us remember Blaser's question: 'Might it not then actually be true that salvation comes from the Jews?'

This is not just a rhetorical question. At a key point, it suggests the direction we must take if we are to achieve a theologically defensible view of salvation. We must look at the *biblical* view of salvation, and in this context, more specifically, the *Old Testament* view of salvation.

17

Salvation Comes from the Jews (Jn. 4:22)

What follows will be simply a trial run-up, an attempt to take our bearings in respect of the biblical view of salvation. In the next chapter we shall have to adopt another approach and concentrate our attention on christology. But in the present context we need a provisional survey from one particular standpoint, that of a multi-dimensional *'geometry of salvation'* — the many different dimensions — of the salvation that 'comes from the Jews'.

Since I wish at the same time to take into account throughout the discussion the ecumenical debates on the theme of 'Salvation Today', particularly the reflection which followed the Bangkok Missionary Conference on that theme in 1973, I shall select from the wealth of biblical material an illustrative passage which played an important part in ecumenical efforts to achieve consensus.

In his main address to the Bangkok Conference, the well-known Indian sociologist and ecumenist Dr. M. M. Thomas took as his starting point for examining the concrete approach and different dimensions of the Old Testament hope of salvation the following passage from the Psalms:

> 'That our sons may grow up as the young plants and that our daughters may be as the polished corner of the Temple.
> That our garners may be full and plenteous with all manner of store;
> That our sheep may bring forth thousands and ten thousands in our streets;
> That our oxen may be strong to labour;
> That there be no leading into captivity,
> and no complaining in our streets.
> Happy are the people that are in such a state.
> Blessed are the people who have the Lord for their God'. (Ps. 144:12-15)[5]

There is no mistaking the extremely concrete, earthy, even 'materialistic' approach here. There is explicit reference to an astonishing range and variety of basic human needs: *biological and physiological*—the youthful vigour of the men and the beauty of the women, the agreeable blessings of physical health and well-being; *economic*—productivity and material abundance, described of course in the terms and images of the hopes entertained by an agrarian society but easily transposable *mutatis mutandis* into those of other economic systems and contexts; even *social and political* needs are not ignored—the longing for a city, a society blessed with peace at home and abroad, in which there is no 'complaining', no threat of foreign aggression, no domestic tyranny or oppression.

M. M. Thomas sums up this vision of salvation as follows, drawing out its contemporary relevance to the needs and aspirations of people in the 'developing countries' especially:

> 'Peoples seeking a richer and fuller realization of the potentialities of their humanity through building a new society which will provide health and plenty, peace and justice—this secular pursuit of happiness is the context within which I must speak of spiritual salvation'.[6]

This touches on another aspect of the Old Testament view of salvation. *Though* the Bible speaks consistently of salvation in terms of basic human needs, even material needs, *though* it never ignores the question of happiness, food, justice and peace and never minimizes the importance of these things for human well-being, and *though* the question of salvation can never be divorced from human well-being and any such divorce would be an abstract view of salvation quite alien to the psalmist and to the Old Testament as a whole, *nevertheless* salvation is not to be equated with well-being or even with the sum-total of satisfied human needs. The biblical witnesses are opposed not only to any abstract idealistic view of salvation but also to any materialistic, pseudo-concrete (i.e. positivistic) identification of well-being and salvation.

This emerges strongly in the almost liturgical conclusion or climax of Psalm 144 and its message of salvation: 'Happy are the people that are in such a state! Blessed are the people who have the Lord for their God!' The horizontal hopes of Israel are inseparably bound up with the vertical dimension, its vision of God. M. M. Thomas calls this vision of God the 'spiritual' dimension of salvation. For him, an Eastern Orthodox thinker, the anthropological aspect of human spirituality is of the utmost importance. Let us firstly attend carefully to what he says:

'Man belongs to the animal species and is involved in the processes and necessities of organic nature. What distinguishes man from the animal is the knowledge that he is so involved. With awareness of a self which, while being involved in nature, also transcends it, goes a sense of responsibility and the search to fulfil it. It is this self-transcendence which is the spiritual freedom and the personal being of man. It does not at any time deny his involvement in the processes of animal nature and its necessities, e.g. hunger or sex, but gives a spiritual quality to it, for the involvement now takes place not within the realm of necessity but within a structure of meaning and sacredness which the self in its freedom of self-transcendence chooses for itself'.[7]

To illustrate the practical consequences for human behaviour if this spiritual dimension is taken into account, M. M. Thomas takes a concrete example from the field of sexual ethics. He quotes the critical question put to the Freudians by an Indian anthropologist, Dr. M. P. John:

'Freudians have said that most, if not all, human actions are coloured by sex broadly defined. We may reverse the statement and say that in man the whole of sexuality is conditioned by humanity, that is, involved with questions of spirit, freedom and sacredness. Nothing that man does can be dissociated from his spirit. Man is not such a combination of spirit and body that certain actions can be considered as exclusively belonging to the body . . . . In all action man acts in his wholeness, and each action may be an exercise of his freedom'.[8]

This brings out clearly the anthropological aspect of spiritual salvation. This Eastern emphasis on spirituality is so important, particularly its ecumenical implications for Western people with their secularized life-style, that it must be taken very seriously in ecumenical discussion.

But as the psalmist sees it, the vertical dimension of salvation has an even deeper significance. We have to interpret it not only anthropologically but also, and above all, theologically, always bearing in mind that the two aspects are inseparable. It is not just a matter of a more profound vision of our existence as persons but also of our vision of God. And not just the vision of God as a general concept or as Transcendence but the vision of a God who is here addressed by his name: the vision of the God of Israel. 'Blessed are the people who have *Yahweh* (the Lord) for their God!' The psalmist's hope of salvation, described and illustrated with such refreshing concreteness and earthiness, has a fixed abode: it is anchored in Yahweh, the God of Israel, the creator of heaven and earth. It is impossible to remain faithful to the Bible and at the same time to speak of an anonymous, arbitrarily interchangeable, symbolic or mythological salvation. We can only speak of salvation by giving it this specific concrete reference and as having this God of Israel as its source and goal.

What practical consequences does this connection, this 'alliance', have for the biblical view of salvation? I wish to point out two such. Firstly, this theological connection, this vertical reference, of salvation helps us to demythologize and radicalize our secular — or our abstract religious — view of salvation. I use the term 'demythologize' to make clear the *relative value* of well-being in the context of salvation by the reference to God. The *intrinsic* value of well-being is not in dispute. It is *good* to be healthy, to delight in beauty, to partake of economic prosperity, to live in peace. It is good to share in such blessings and, as an essential part of sharing them, to strive for them as desirable goals. We are not entitled to ignore the concrete terms of the psalmist's hymn of praise nor, least of all, to tone down or belittle their theological importance. Such blessings are God's *good* gifts. But they are not more than that. As *God's* good gifts they are not to be regarded in any sense as *divine,* as putting salvation into our keeping. Their value is the unquestionably positive secular value of well-being but not the mythological positivistic value of either secular or religious salvation.

This clarification, it seems to me, is most important. There is always a danger of making idols of life's blessings, either by the religious apotheosis

22

of pagan mythologies or by the secular transposition of relatively valid value-judgements into absolute and final values. What can be endorsed as a *means* to a true life in freedom is turned into an *end in itself*. God's good gift becomes an idol. This can be illustrated from precisely those blessings on which the psalmist meditates. How easily the body, beauty, health, for example, are identified with human 'hopes of salvation' and their value hopelessly inflated and distorted in consequence. We are offered vitalistic gospels of salvation promising the solution of all our problems if only we give uninhibited rein to our sensuality and sexuality. Such gospels clearly promise more than they can deliver. The same applies to economic and political doctrines of salvation. Whenever a false status is accorded to positive ideals in our physical, economic or political life, the true significance of these ideals is endangered. The vertical dimension of biblical salvation, the biblical vision of God, protects human freedom from our human temptation to idolatry — both our own and that of other people. It demythologizes secular (or religious) salvation and in doing so brings out its true value all the more clearly.

As a definition of the distinctive feature of the Christian attitude to earthly blessings, the term *'eschatological proviso'* has enjoyed a certain popularity in recent theology. Christians, the argument goes, should adopt Paul's principle of 'having as having not', formulated by the apostle in reference to marriage: 'Married men should live as though they were not married' (1 Cor. 7:29). This principle was given a prominent place in the work of Rudolf Bultmann in particular, being regarded by him almost as a basic principle of ethics. In the Bultmann school it has usually been referred to as the 'desecularization' *(Entweltlichung)* tendency in the true Christian view of salvation. It has to be acknowledged that there is some New Testament support for this emphasis. But I would want to enter a caveat against any unduly systematic use of this formula. The 'desecularization' of salvation is a highly ambiguous formulation. Like the concept of the 'eschatological proviso', it seems to me far too negative. Above all, it encourages an idealistic understanding (i.e. *mis*understanding) of salvation. It makes it all too easy for us to remove salvation to the 'inner world' of faith and to relegate the 'external world' of concrete things and actions to the 'outer darkness' of the unreal. The view of salvation is not merely demythologized but even dematerialized, or at any rate de-politicized. But the biblical hope of salvation provides no support whatever for such a process, least of all the Old Testament witness to that hope. The psalmist's shining vision of God certainly meant for him no clouding over of the 'horizontal horizon'. On the contrary, it brings it all the more clearly into view.

The vision of God also *radicalizes* the question of salvation. I use this term to try to indicate another of the practical implications of the indissoluble connection between redemption and God. The vision of God broadens and deepens the scope of the question of salvation. The question always remains, of course, a question addressed to me as an individual person. 'How do I find a gracious God?' as Luther properly asked. And it certainly would be no distortion of the psalmist's thought to say that the question of God undoubtedly arises at the very heart of all my problems and needs as an individual person. Salvation concerns my health, my delight in what is lovely and of good report, my economic and political hopes. In some of the psalms this simple personal individual dimension of the question of salvation and well-being is presented directly; for example, in Psalm 30, one of the biblical passages studied at Bangkok, and in many others. In this sense, too, when it is a question of 'Salvation Today', there is nothing to stop us from beginning, and indeed everything to constrain us to begin, quite concretely by saying *mea res agitur*. The only 'today' any of us has is always also our own personal today.

Here as elsewhere, however, there is a world of difference between really being concrete and the illusion of being concrete. In the diversified perspective of Psalm 144 especially, the *illusion of being concrete* will mean a fixation on superficial common interests, living salvation atomistically, thinking of 'today' as meaning only my needs and concerns as a private citizen, leaving out of account the overall horizon of our common 'today' and ultimately the eschatological 'Today' of God (2 Cor. 6:2). The psalmist bars the way to such a view of salvation. His approach is really concrete; it includes precisely this ecumenical and eschatological horizon. There is nothing illusory about his concreteness.

In this connection, too, the final verse is vitally important: 'Blessed are the people who have the Lord for their God!' Here the psalmist speaks of *the people of God* and of *God the Lord*. Far from existing in its own right, the psalmist's hope of salvation—so intensely personal and individual—exists within the framework of this covenant which embraces the people of God and God himself the Lord. This radicalizes the biblical view of salvation. 'Private happiness' is not crushed but it is certainly broken open, opened up. From the standpoint of the Bible, it is impossible to find a 'gracious God' for oneself alone; to seek the gracious God, we must necessarily seek him for our fellow human beings, for the world. From the biblical standpoint, the question of my own happiness is at the same time that of the happiness of the people of God and of all the peoples of the earth.

Here the concept of God becomes relevant to our praxis. Or, rather, not the 'concept' of God, not the abstract notion of divinity, for even with that we could still keep the world at a distance, but he God whom the psalmist names: God the Lord, Yahweh, the God of the Jews, or, in Christian language, the God and Father of our Lord Jesus Christ. *This* God is the God of all human beings, my God who is at the same time *our* Father and Creator of *all* that is. The necessary corollary of linking salvation indissolubly with his name, provided we do so with the requisite faith and not just paying hypocritical lip-service ('Lord! Lord!'), is movement in the direction of our fellow human beings, the practical 'ecumenism' which corresponds to this name, loving concern for the near and the far.

Once this connection is effected between the Yahweh, the name Jesus Christ, on the one hand, and salvation and happiness on the other, any restriction of *this* salvation and *this* happiness to the private sphere is ruled out. Far from diluting our commitment in the world, this spirituality, as a dimension of salvation, actually radicalizes this commitment. Berdyaev's frequently quoted epigram that whereas the problem of my own bread is a material question the question of bread for my neighbour is a spiritual one helps us to see, as the religious socialists clearly saw, that the spirit of Jesus, the Holy Spirit, actually constrains us to practice a 'holy materialism' by radicalizing our vision of salvation and happiness. Instead of needlessly complicating the real 'horizontal' situation, this vertical reference in fact sets it in a refreshingly deep and broad perspective. The question of God is not a superfluous or secondary question in the general context of the problem of salvation and happiness, even today. Perhaps less than ever today in view of the dangers of one-dimensional thought and practice in our secularized life. The question of God and it alone provides the basis for a biblically satisfactory (and liberating) 'geometry of salvation'.

Towards a Fully Ecumenical Salvation
To sum up the argument so far: in the light of the Bible, salvation cannot be reduced to a single dimension. Salvation is not a one-dimensional reality but a multi-dimensional one. It is necessary, therefore, to examine critically any attempt to present salvation as one-dimensional whether it is a transposition of the 'horizontal' into the 'vertical' or of the 'vertical' into the 'horizontal'. Salvation is an event with many facets.

Put positively, in the light of the Bible, our witness to salvation must be 'comprehensive', 'holistic' and 'ecumenical'. 'Sectarianism' in any form is heresy in the truest sense of the word; the division, indeed the destruction, of salvation.

At first sight, nothing of any great moment seems to be gained by this emphatic statement, and of course it needs to be developed in greater detail. Yet, even as it stands, it is already a contribution to our understanding of salvation. Salvation is 'healing' in the universal sense. This insight has both anthropological and cosmological implications. Salvation understood in this way resists all attempts and every temptation to explain the world, or to master it one-dimensionally. It underlines the fact that humanity —and the creation—are not just one-dimensional

27

objects of our theory and praxis. We can and should, of course, study human life and the world thoroughly in all their different aspects and draw conclusions from our researches. But to do this in a really intelligent and helpful way, we must resist all forms of scientific, ideological and political totalitarianism; in other words, all attempts to interpret and manipulate our world exclusively in terms of one or other dimension. If it remains true to this holistic view of salvation, theology will be able to make its own modest, critical yet constructive contribution.

It seems to me that there is a growing sense of the need for this 'wholeness' and 'comprehensiveness' in ecumenical theology today. The ecumenical movement with its deep concern for the unity and mission of Christians also has an important part to play here. The very diversity of the different confessional families of Christians, with their diverse emphases in soteriology prevents the establishment of any one-sided view of salvation. The conflict between the 'horizontalists' and the 'verticalists', ugly though it may be in certain cases, has in the last analysis helped us to remain aware of the different dimensions and the wholeness of salvation in our continuing ecumenical discussion. This is a healthy safeguard against the acceptance of a premature consensus. It also excludes any crude syncretism. Positively, it corrects rigidities in belief and practice; it fosters sensitivity and openness to different ways of bearing our common witness to holistic salvation and introduces us to the ecumenical geometry of salvation.

Let me conclude this chapter with an ecumenical statement on this theme: 'The salvation which Christ brought and in which we participate offers a comprehensive wholeness in this divided life. We

28

understand salvation as newness of life — the unfolding of true humanity in the fulness of God (Col. 2:9). It is salvation of the soul and the body, of the individual and society, mankind and "the groaning creation" (Rom. 8:19) . . . . Therefore we see the struggles for economic justice, political freedom and cultural renewal as elements in the total liberation of the world through the mission of God. This liberation is finally fulfilled when "death is swallowed up in victory" (1 Cor. 15:55). This comprehensive notion of salvation demands of the whole of the people of God a matching comprehensive approach to their participation in salvation'.[9]

2

The Centre of Salvation

Salvation in No Other Name!

In the last chapter we were concerned with the dimensions of salvation. It was vital to resist and exclude from the very start any unilateral, one-dimensional view of salvation. The wholeness of the biblical view of salvation was established. Now we must try to state this truth more precisely by moving on from the discussion of the various dimensions of salvation to the consideration of its centre. We shall be concerned in this chapter with the question of *the centre of salvation*. Put this question to the New Testament witnesses and their response is unanimous: the centre of salvation is found in the name, the person and the work and life of *Jesus Christ*. These witnesses see in the event of Christ the fulfilment of time, the centre of the history of salvation: 'When the right time finally came, God sent his own Son' (Gal. 4:4). In Jesus Christ the final seal was set on the solidarity of the Creator with his creation: 'The Word became a human being and, full of grace and truth, lived among us. We saw his glory, the glory which he received as God's only Son' (Jn. 1:14). Here, then, is the foundation of salvation: 'For God has already placed Jesus Christ as the one and only foundation, and no other foundation can be laid' (1 Cor. 3:11). On this point above all, the apostolic preaching is categorical and clear from the very beginning: 'There is no salvation in anyone else at all, for there is no other name under heaven granted to men, by which we may receive salvation' (Acts 4:12, NEB).

These well-known words reflect the basic direction of the entire New Testament message. A variety of formulas may be used and different accents heard but the indissoluble link between salvation and this name, this person, this history, is no 'variable' but a 'constant', *the* constant of the New Testament, the *cantus firmus* of its polyphonic testimony.

This basic direction is characteristic not only of the theory but also of the practice of the original Christian movement. In the first place, of its *praxis pietatis,* its liturgical and cultic life: 'In all congregations *Jesus Christ* was worshipped as *the bringer of salvation.* It is he who is confessed in baptism, he who is worshipped in the cult as the present *Kurios,* he who is awaited as the coming Judge and Saviour' (Bultmann).[10] But the same basis underlies the missionary work of Christians. Certainly in presenting the Gospel to their near and distant audiences Christian missionaries were ready to be Jews to the Jews and Greeks to the Greeks (1 Cor. 9:20 ff.), i.e. to enter with sympathy and understanding into the cultural and intellectual situations of their fellow human-beings, but at no time did this imply any possibility of detaching their message of salvation from the quite concrete figure and history attested in the New Testament or relativizing the name of Jesus Christ.

So it was that within the exuberant bewilderingly diverse religious market of late Hellenistic society, something quite unique appeared; something which, considering the generally accepted rules of the trade in salvations and saviours, adopted a surprisingly inflexible line. The salvation proclaimed by Christians has clear articulate historical features. It is salvation with an unmistakably human face, that of Jesus of Nazareth. To most of their contemporaries, whether religious or atheist, the missionary strategy of the Christians seemed scandalous or foolish, unfair competition, proof of the primitive character of the Christian religion. Even in the Church, attempts were made quite early on to modify this 'rigid line'. But the basic apostolic writings effectively barred the way to any slide into syncretism. In the experience of salvation and, above all, in the witness to salvation, there was no bypassing the categorical New Testament affirmations: 'There is no salvation in anyone else at all . . . . ' 'There is no other name . . . . by which we may receive salvation'.

This insistence on Jesus Christ as the centre of salvation is sometimes described as the 'exclusiveness' of the Christian faith. Depending on the point of view, this is either stressed and affirmed, or, more commonly today, rejected as 'intolerance'. But the term 'exclusive' is misleading. It suggests an arrogant claim to monopoly and sounds aggressive and inquisitorial. Such attitudes are discredited among intelligent people today and, with them, the term 'exclusiveness' as well. This mistrust is well-founded. One will search the history of the Church and theology a long time to find a more dangerous temptation than the temptation to exclusiveness in the bad sense of the term, i.e. the tendency to exclude others, to break off relations with them and to anathematize them on the ground of a supposed superior understanding or, worse still, in a spirit of self-righteousness. Any such tendency must be resisted not only on grounds of common humanity but also for fundamental theological reasons. Wherever this tendency prevails, the Gospel is all too easily turned into a law, the universal invitation of the Good News of the sovereign love of God into a dissuasive threat.

'There is no salvation in anyone else at all . . . . .' Is this affirmation of faith a claim to exclusiveness in the bad sense? I think not. To interpret it in this way would be to draw wrong conclusions from the fact that salvation is rooted in christology. We must distinguish here, I believe, between *'christomonism'* and a 'christological concentration'. By 'christomonism' I mean the tendency to reduce the rich diversity of biblical themes to the name 'Jesus Christ' and then to turn to the world and to relate this name to the rich diversity of human history as a whole in a primarily defensive and exclusive way.

Such a position, it seems to me, would be an utter travesty of the biblical record of Christ's life and work. The history of Christ takes a quite different direction. It is not the story of a coup achieved by some self-centred religious personality seeking to bring everyone and everything under one umbrella, his own. What we are offered here is the story of how God set out on a mission which embraces the whole of humanity across all the frontiers. In Jesus Christ — the Jesus Christ whom believers confess as the one and only Saviour — 'there is no such thing as Jew and Greek, slave and freeman, male and female' (Gal. 3:28). The salvation which is anchored in christology is universal in its scope. 'God our Saviour . . . . wants everyone to be saved and to come to know the truth' (I Tim. 2:4). This position is faithfully reflected in the ancient Church's doctrine of Christ. God became a human being, not a Christian.

33

A reductionist christomonism must be clearly distinguished from the missionary and theological programme of a *'christological concentration'*, as developed so impressively in recent times by Karl Barth. The aim here is to prevent the liberating and binding centre of salvation from dissolving into an arbitrary syncretism or a helpless relativism; to preserve its identity, rather, to bring out its implications and highlight them in the contemporary context. That seems to me a sensible programme for mission and theology, provided there is no arrogant idea of enhancing its own image by complacently or proudly differentiating itself from the rest. Any such notion would only, I repeat, reveal our contempt for the actual concrete history of Jesus, its evangelical message and pattern, and demonstrate that the last thing our thought and action was concentrated on was Christ! The object here, on the contrary, is to remain true to the distinctively *Christian* dimension in the interests of *all* humanity.

Admittedly this theological approach rests on a specific assumption. It assumes that this distinctive Christian element is valuable, that in the saving event of Jesus Christ something decisive and indispensable has been revealed, something of ultimate concern to every human being, namely, their salvation. The tension between this 'prejudice' or 'assumption' and its open and unprejudiced consequences is the life-breath of the witness of Christian theology to the exclusive yet inclusive centre of salvation.

To my mind, this tension finds clear and helpful expression in 1 Tim. 4:10 especially. We find here the following paradoxical statement about the God of hope and salvation: ' . . . . who is the Saviour of all and especially of those who believe'. Both parts

34

of this dialectical affirmation must be heeded. First the adverb *'especially'*. Salvation in Christ is no 'preliminary hearing' where a merely 'preliminary attitude' would be in order. The attitude we adopt to it is not a matter of no consequence. This salvation calls for a definite response, a corresponding commitment, a responding faith. But this 'exclusive' (a better word would be 'committed') response cannot be regarded as exclusive in the pejorative sense, least of all as claiming a Christian monopoly of salvation. Christians have no such monopoly. The God of our hope is the *'Saviour of all'*. If we think of salvation as a possession we misunderstand it completely. A credible witness to salvation is only possible when our attitude to our fellow human beings, irrespective of race, culture, class or sex, is one of unqualified openness. Salvation in Christ requires of us an *open-ended* theory and praxis of salvation.

Starting from this christological centre, how are we to achieve a more precise theological description of salvation? My approach to this question will be in three steps:

(1)   an examination of the concept of salvation in biblical theology;
(2)   an attempt to elucidate the theological significance of the name 'Jesus Christ'; and
(3)   a systematic theological consideration of the 'doctrine of the three offices of Christ'.

The Biblical Concept of Salvation

I have argued in favour of a christological concentration on the centre of salvation, one which is not christomonist. In the present context this means that, while anchored in christology, the Christian view of salvation cannot be isolated from the Old Testament use of the term 'salvation'. We find no such isolation in the New Testament for all its concentration of salvation in Christ. This redemption is repeatedly connected up with Old Testament promises; in the gospels, especially Matthew, but also in the other apostolic writings. The 'new covenant' in Christ can only be understood against the background of the 'old covenant'. Here again we have to remember that 'salvation comes from the Jews' — the 'centre of salvation' has an Old Testament prelude.

The main Old Testament word for 'to save', 'to heal', 'to rescue' is *jasha'* (noun *jeshua'*). Its root meaning is 'to be roomy, broad' as opposed especially to 'being oppressed' i.e. being hemmed in, constricted, confined.[11] The afflicted and the oppressed are rescued, new opportunities of living are opened up to them, and in this way they experience salvation. This not only refers to individual distress, as frequently in the Psalms, but also to collective distress. Pushed to the wall, God's people is saved from the enemies who oppress it. This is the way of salvation. Although this act of deliverance can be attributed to human agents, it becomes increasingly clear in the Old Testament that the real deliverer is Yahweh himself. In the end, it is only God himself 'by the power of his right hand' who can really deliver his 'anointed', his people, the individual psalmist. Hence the burden of the psalmist's praise of salvation is: 'Some trust in their war chariots and others in their horses, but we trust in the power of the Lord our God' (Ps. 20:7). Israel's entire history is understood as a history of salvation and liberation, despite the manifest evils of human — only too human — history. One of the shortest Old Testament confessions of faith is 'The Lord saves', the 'God of our salvation'.

What is God's people saved *from?* The answer has

just been indicated: it is saved from its enemies and oppressors in history, as above all, and paradigmatically for all the rest, it was saved in the events of the Exodus. Salvation therefore has both historical and social dimensions. The socially oppressed are frequently promised deliverance. In his saving action, God takes up their cause: 'Because he defends the poor man and saves him from those who condemn him to death' (Ps. 109:31). But the concept of salvation cannot be limited to the social and the historical. It is deliverance in the widest possible sense. 'There is deliverance from the perils of sickness, imprisonment or hostility, whether these come alone or accompany or are the effect of other oppressions. In each case the dangers mean a weakening of strength and are thus a foretaste of the death which overpowers the oppressed. Hence deliverance is salvation from death. Trust in this salvation and help of God from all the tribulations and terrors to which man is subject and which . . . . always and everywhere oppress him, is an essential element in the believer's self-understanding'.[12]

This is a quite concrete, down-to-earth, historical approach to salvation. Yet it embraces more than the area of collective and individual history. Salvation has a 'protological' dimension and, above all, an 'eschatological' one. The experience of salvation in the events of the Exodus, for example, points back to the beginning and forward to the end of history. To the beginning, when Yahweh, the true Creator of all things, rescued his creation from the clutches of the forces of chaos (Ps. 74:12ff.); to the end, for *jasha* very early came to mean deliverance, help and salvation in the last days. 'The deliverance which makes salvation possible is preservation from the eschatological onset of the peoples (Zech. 12:7). But, above all, it is the gathering and bringing home of the dispersed from the whole world (Is. 43:5-7; Jer. 31:7; 46:27; Zeph. 3:19; Zech. 8:7; Ps. 106:47). By his helpful intervention (Is. 59:1; Zech. 8:13), therefore, God inaugurates the eschatological age'.[13] God consistently demonstrates to his prophet that He is liberator and helper in every need and distress: 'The Lord says: "I am the Lord your God, who led you out of Egypt. You have no God but me. I alone am your saviour . . . . ' (Hos. 13:4).

But this time of the end, which as the time of salvation is also inseparably connected with the coming Messiah (Ps. 91:11-16; Is. 49:6, 8; 61:10; Jer. 23:6) and indeed with his sufferings (Is. 53), is not to be understood as a time of salvation for this one people *alone,* however intimately it is, of course, connected with this people; the promise of judgement and salvation applies also to the other peoples (Is. 45:23ff.; 49:8-12; 60:1-12). In this final vision, too, the 'exclusive' salvation of Israel is 'universal' in its thrust.

The Old Testament view of salvation is presupposed, adopted and — with a concentrated focus on and inseparable connection with the name, person and history of Jesus Christ — further unfolded in the *New Testament*. We shall have to examine this development more closely when we consider New Testament christology and the soteriological concepts of Christian dogmatics. At this first step in our reflections, however, I wish to point out how, according to the gospels, Jesus assimilates the Old Testament view of salvation and how the Old Testament assumptions and themes persist throughout the New Testament. This seems to me extremely important in view of the weakening of the Hebraic tradition and the reinforcement of the Hellenistic tradition in the historical development of Christian theology, both in the earliest period and in the later history of the Church. In the present context this led to a 'spiritualization' of salvation alien to the New Testament approach, particularly as represented in the synoptic gospels.

The New Testament term for salvation is *soteria,* while the verb 'to heal', 'to save', is *sozein.* In both cases the reference can be to rescue or deliverance from danger and death (Mt. 8:25; 14:30; 27:40, 42, 48; Mk. 3:4; 15:30; Lk. 6:9; 23:35, 37, 39; Acts 27:20, 31, 34; Heb. 11:7), from sickness (Mt. 9:21; Mk. 5:23, 28; 6:56; Lk. 8:36; Jn. 11:12; Acts 4:9; 14:9), from fear of death (Jn. 12:27), from oppression by enemies (Acts 7:25). The term is frequently used of the miracles of Jesus where it refers to the healing of particular infirmities as the form of the help given by Jesus to sick and oppressed individuals. But salvation is attested not only in the concrete works of Jesus, particularly his healings; it is at the same time the *meaning and purpose* of his entire life, ministry and sufferings. The song of Zechariah in Luke's prologue gives a pointer to the purpose of Jesus' life: he is to 'save us from our enemies, from the power of all those who hate us' (Lk. 1:71) and also 'to tell his people that they will be saved' (Lk. 1:77). So too in the prologue to Matthew's gospel, the name of Jesus foreshadows his life's work as the history of our salvation: 'he will save his people from their sins' (Mt. 1:21). Jesus himself sees his mission in similar terms: 'The Son of Man came to seek and to save the lost' (Lk. 19:10).

In these passages, the *eschatological dimension* of salvation is envisaged, once again against the background of the Old Testament. Redemption, deliverance, is seen in the perspective of the coming kingdom of God, in the context of the final crisis and judgement which the coming of that kingdom signifies for us as human beings. Salvation then means the opposite of damnation (Lk. 9:56; Mk. 16:16), destruction and death (Mt. 18:11), condemnation and wrath (Jn. 3:17; 12:47). Salvation ultimately means entry into the kingdom of God (Mt. 19:24f.; Mk. 10:24-26; Lk. 18:25f.), or, in Johannine terms, eternal life (Jn. 5:24; 17:2).

These two terms, the synoptic term 'kingdom of God' and the Johannine term 'eternal life', are central for soteriology and reflect an important characteristic of the formal structure of the New Testament view of salvation, namely, the typical *dialectic between future and present dimensions* of salvation. For Jesus and his disciples the kingdom of God is the coming reality, the ultimate eschatological goal not immediately available to us at present but solely God's to withhold or bestow. Correspondingly, the term 'life' (*zoe*), which is closely related to the term *soteria* in the New Testament and especially in the Johannine writings, also points to the eschatological fulfilment of salvation, the final deliverance from death, to eternity.

But the New Testament eschatological hope is never just a future 'opium of the people', never a mere promise with a purely otherworldly or supra-temporal reference having nothing whatever to do with the present times in which we live. The kingdom comes, intrudes into our present time, affects the actual reality of life now, sets present conditions in movement. It does this, moreover, by encouraging and summoning us in the light of the future reality of the coming kingdom of God to follow the example of Jesus by seriously and committedly establishing 'signs of the kingdom', 'signs of life' already here and now. In this sense the kingdom is already in our midst, eminently present.

Nor is eternal life simply redemption after death; it is salvation already shining on us and liberating us today. 'Whoever believes in the Son *has* eternal life' (Jn. 3:36). And for John, too, 'having' does not mean outright possession, so to speak, but always means at the same time the call to the corresponding decision, the test of present discipleship.

This dialectic between the 'not yet' and the 'already now' is fundamental to the New Testament view of salvation, life and even of the world. We find it fully respected in the New Testament letters, especially in those of Paul. True, 'statements predominate in which *salvation is conceived as a thing of the future.* It is for "salvation" that Christ will someday appear for the benefit of those who await him (Heb. 9:28), who, by the power of God through faith are preserved "for a salvation ready to be revealed in the last time" (1 Pet. 1:5; cf. 1:9; 2:2). . . . Life is likewise often spoken of *as a life that is yet to come* — for instance when the "crown of life" is promised (Rev. 2:10; Jas. 1:12), or in the expression "hope of life (eternal)" (Tit. 1:2 . . . .)'.[14] Yet here again, this eschatological salvation quite clearly intervenes very concretely in our life here and now and profoundly transforms our human situation in relation both to God and our fellow human beings. Believers, it is insisted, are *hoi sozomenoi* ('those who are being saved' Acts 2:47) or even *hoi sesosmenoi* ('those who have been saved' Eph. 2:8). The power of fate and the cosmic forces and powers has been already broken, even if for the time being they have certainly not just disappeared or been liquidated. They still oppress believers and we must not underestimate them; yet they can no longer separate us from the love of God revealed in Jesus Christ. 'For it was in hope that we were saved' (Rom. 8:24).[15] This statement refers not just to an

41

ongoing present but also to a completed past, yet certainly not denoting some static condition but including an imperative and excluding all fatalism and conferring the right and the power to live in hope already here and now.

This is the distinctive character of the apostolic view of salvation: it has *this* direction and *this* tension. With Bultmann, we can define its content as follows: 'The salvation wrought by Christ's sacrifice is generally termed forgiveness of sin, release (*apolutrosis*, "redemption"), rightwising ("justification"), sanctification, or purification, when it is being described in its effect upon believers. . . . In addition, it is termed victory over the cosmic powers, especially over death'. . . .[16] The many dimensions of the apostolic view of salvation are clearly reflected in this summary, though I believe it possible to take it further, especially with reference to the concrete embodiments of salvation as regularly envisaged by Paul, above all in the paranetic or ethical sections of his epistles. Eschatological salvation illuminates all areas of human life. Above all, it inspires Christians with the will to live accordingly in every area of their lives, including their relations with their fellow human beings, their family life, their work and even their political life. It is instructive to find, for example, that the notorious thirteenth chapter of *Romans* in particular should refer to the eschatological horizon of its intense hope of salvation: 'You must do this, because you know that the time has come for you to wake up from your sleep. For the moment when we will be saved is closer now than it was when we first believed' (Rom. 13:11). An alert intelligence and activity, a keen awareness of political realities, these are a vital part of the theory — and practice — of salvation.

No description of the New Testament view of

salvation would be complete without one further final specification. The New Testament writers are very emphatic that this many-sided salvation is not a floating, unmoored, homeless and nameless blessing. They do not leave vague and undefined the basis of this reality of salvation (*soteria*) and of our knowledge of it. Salvation, for them, means the person, the history and the name of Jesus Christ. It is to be understood in the light of this specific centre. Here especially the New Testament witnesses are unequivocal. They may differ considerably in their views of salvation, in the emphasis they place on its different material aspects, but in respect of the embodiment of redemption, the author of salvation, they are quite unanimous and unhesitant. There is no room for anonymity here. There is no mistaking the name: Jesus Christ. Salvation is '*en Christo*' as this frequently employed formula constantly reminds us. In other words, salvation is his work. To enquire into salvation in the Christian sense of the term, therefore, means that we must consider not only the biblical concept of salvation but also the name and saving work of Jesus Christ. The next two sections of this chapter will therefore be devoted to this investigation.

The Name of Jesus Christ: Its Significance for Salvation

I remind you once again of the unequivocal New Testament assertion concerning salvation: 'There is no salvation in anyone else at all, for there is no other name under heaven granted to men, by which we may receive salvation' (Acts 4:12). The striking thing about this confession of faith, which forms the kernel of one of the first (stylized) Christian sermons, is the way it attaches the Gospel as the message of salvation to one quite specific name. In the Christian

43

view, salvation is not something anonymous and abstract. Theologians have talked a good deal in recent years of an 'anonymous Christianity' (K. Rahner, H. Ott). Their concern here was to bar any restriction of salvation to an established institution of salvation and to defend Christ's sovereignty over the visible Church. But is this really a very helpful term? Could it not lend countenance to the erroneous notion that a 'Christianity without Christ' is possible? In the light of the New Testament, however, any such idea is ruled out. Undoubtedly there is a Christ without Christianity, in the sense that Christ's presence and sovereignty transcend the boundaries of Christendom, and still more those of 'Christian civilization'. But there is no Christianity without Christ. The identity of Christian existence is indissolubly bound up with this name. The terms used have to be taken literally: *Christ*ianity without *Christ* is nothing. This name Christ — and ultimately this name alone — is in reality the 'distinguishing mark of Christianity', the *proprium christianum,* to use the more expressive Latin term. This needs to be remembered also and above all when we seek to understand and bear witness to salvation in the Christian sense.

What does it mean, this attachment of salvation to a particular name, to *this* particular name? This is not something immediately intelligible to us today. All of us start here with a *nominalist cast of mind* — a mentality for which terms and names are just conventional instruments of speech and communication, in contrast to the realist Platonic approach for which terms and even names possess a highly metaphysical quality. Although biblical thinking is neither nominalist nor realist in this sense, it is nevertheless marked by a profound sense of the importance of names. The name is far more than a

44

mere conventional, arbitrary *flatus vocis,* 'sound and fury'. 'What's in a name?' demanded Shakespeare's Juliet. The biblical answer is that the name is laden with the mystery of its bearer's unique personality and, in many important instances, with a great deal more than this, i.e. when it expresses a real programme for the life of its bearer, a real manifesto. Hence the reverence for the name: unequivocally and supremely, of course, for the divine name (we need only recall the Third Commandment) but under the protection of this divine name, also for all human names, too. For biblical thinking, *'nomen est omen',* but more even than that, it is the inalienable, irreplaceable essence and presence of the reality of the person who bears it.

This is true without qualification of the name of Jesus Christ in the New Testament. This name represents the authoritative presence of the person and history it denotes. And at the same time it expresses the basic features of the historical programme of salvation of this 'centre of salvation'. This is not meant in any magical sense at all. Historical and even 'accidental' elements are inseparably connected with this name, an aspect which we shall have to emphasize in connection with the name 'Jesus', and, indeed, in profound consonance with the salvation in Christ. For this salvation in Christ is historically anchored, moulded and even determined in part by history. Yet the eschatological authority and reality of this historical salvation is also attested: it is God's initiative in the 'centre of time', the 'event of salvation' the ultimate significance of which is utterly remote from all arbitrariness. In the biblical perspective, therefore, the name Jesus Christ sets the course for the witness to salvation. To investigate the significance of this name, therefore, is also important for us.

We begin with the second element in the name: *Christ*. According to the testimony of the apostles, Christian salvation is defined, above all, by this name, with the formula *'en Christo'*. The name 'Christ' is a title, of course, and it is here that the programmatic feature referred to earlier becomes unmistakable. In the conjunction 'Jesus Christ' it is more than just a title, of course. Very early on, in both Christian and non-Christian usage, it became a personal name. The terms 'Christian' and 'Christianity' are completely derivative from this name and from the very beginning they used it not as a general title but as a name for the unique person Jesus Christ identified with it. We shall do well to remember this inseparable connection between title and name: the personal and functional components of salvation are inseparable. The person and the work are intimately interrelated here. Considerable importance attaches to this circumstance for our understanding of salvation or, in dogmatic terminology, for the christological aspect of all soteriology.

Essentially, however, 'Christ' is a title, indeed a very distinctive one. *Christos* is the Greek translation of the Hebrew *mashiah*. This at once points us unmistakably in a specific direction, that of the world of the Old Testament, the Jewish world. The word means 'the anointed' and is applied to those dignitaries who, according to the Old Testament, were customarily 'anointed' in Israel: the priests, certain of the prophets, and, above all, the kings. Yahweh's anointed acquires special significance in connection with the promise of the eternal Davidic kingdom: 'I have made a covenant with the man I chose; I have promised my servant David, "A descendant of yours will always be king; I will preserve your dynasty for ever"' (Ps. 89:3f.). Here the Messiah is gradually becoming the repository of his people's eschatological hope. This messianic hope became particularly intense in times of oppression, assuming extremely fervent and occasionally aggressive forms. The political and soteriological dimensions of this hope, the expectation of victory over Israel's enemies, and the apotheosis and sanctification of Jerusalem were combined together (with special intensity in the intertestamental period, e.g. in the *Psalms of Solomon*).[17]

When we read the synoptic gospels, what immediately strikes us is the reticence of Jesus himself in the use of the title of Messiah. He seems hardly ever to have used it of himself. When confronted with it, he shows no evident eagerness to accept it as such. He gives an evasive answer to Caiaphas' question (Mk. 14:61f.) and so too before Pilate (Mk. 15:2f.). In the key episode at Caesarea Philippi (Mk. 8:27ff.), though not repudiating Peter's messianic confession, he nevertheless prefers, as he does before Caiaphas, to use another honorific title in his answer, that of the 'Son of Man'. And when Peter wants to repudiate the idea of suffering implicit in this title as used by Jesus, Jesus vigorously repudiates Peter himself with his 'Get away from me, Satan!'

How are we to explain this reticence on Jesus' part? Oscar Cullmann offers a convincing answer to this question in his book on 'Christology': What prompted this suspicion of the title 'Messiah' was not the title itself as such but the widely held triumphalist notion of a political Messiah associated with it, the kind of notion expressed not only in the *Psalms of Solomon* but also in the aspirations of

Jesus' own contemporaries, quite understandably in view of the Roman tyranny.[18] But from the very outset of his ministry, Jesus clearly rejected any interpretation of his mission in terms of power politics. This is evident from the temptation narrative (Lk. 4:1-13), and throughout his ministry Jesus acted and suffered in precisely the same way. 'If rule is for Him a constitutive part of Messiahship, He actualized it in ministry. The way of the Messiah is to dominion through battle and victory; that of Jesus is marked by suffering and defeat . . . . In the ministering lordship which includes suffering and which is based on the thinking of God's thoughts . . . . there dawns a new concept of Messiahship. This prevents Jesus from letting Himself be called the Messiah, since if He were it could only promote misunderstanding of his mission'.[19]

But precisely by taking this line, Jesus linked up with the profoundest Old Testament traditions concerning the true role and hope of God's people and the coming of God's kingdom. Instead of copying the despotism of earthly kingdoms, this kingdom follows the path of self-sacrificial solidarity with all human beings, above all with the poor and oppressed. It is the rule of love and justice. Of *this* kingdom Jesus was the authoritative representative. By words and deeds of liberating love, he embodied the will of God. In this sense he was the true Messiah and undoubtedly understood himself to be, as such, the one in whom the promises of the history of salvation are fulfilled. Although this title was not used by Jesus directly, his disciples nevertheless adopted it after the resurrection, purified and given new meaning by Jesus, as if to do so was the most natural thing in the world. It was indeed difficult for them to do anything else, since in fact the promise of God's saving eschatological presence had

48

for them been fulfilled in Jesus. Thus it came about that, in the New Testament as in the original Christian communities, the affirmation sounded out with ever-growing conviction: 'Christ Jesus! The Messiah is Jesus! Jesus is the Messiah!' This title and this personal name became so indissolubly connected that they eventually were welded together to form the single name: Jesus Christ.

What is there to learn from this title concerning the nature of Jesus' mission? The first point to be considered, I think, is the intimate connection between it and the hopes of Israel. The context in which Jesus appeared is unmistakably that of the history of salvation, the covenant between Yahweh and his people. He is the heir to the promises of salvation made to Israel. He is the mediator of the new covenant. He steps into the yawning chasm repeatedly opened up in the history of the covenant by Israel's faithlessness, becomes himself the victim of this faithlessness and disobedience, and by his own faithfulness bridges the chasm separating God and humanity, becomes the 'atoner', the 'reconciler' in the deepest sense of the word.

As a result, his life and, above all, his death and resurrection move into the very centre of the original Christian message. Jesus not only linked up with but also deepened the Old Testament hope of salvation by combining with his words and his life the readiness to suffer sacrificially and even to die on the cross. This nonplussed those closest to him; the disciples repeatedly rebelled against this messianic demand. Even for Jesus himself it was no mere matter of course but a decision calling for constant renewal in face of temptation. Yet it was also the basic decision of his life's work, at the very latest from the time of his baptism onwards (the direct linking of the temptation narrative with the story of

Jesus' baptism is significant), renewed right up to the very end at Calvary. Only by the Easter events did it become clear to the disciples that this decision, far from being the pseudo-messianic extravagance of an eccentric masochist, was indeed the true messianic way before God and the nations. This, at least, is how the resurrection is at once interpreted by its witnesses—Jesus' resurrection is the confirmation of his messiahship (Acts 2:36; Rom. 1:4; 1 Tim. 3:16). 'The resurrection is the vindication of Jesus, proof of the legitimacy of his messianic claim, the centre of his work of salvation. The risen Lord is therefore the (true) Messiah of Israel, the one who brings and fulfils the kingdom of God, the one who brings the new world to be finally established at his second coming, the Lord of his faithful ones who trust him, believe in him, hope for him and live in him'.[20]

Allow me to return once more in the present (soteriological) context to the pregnant formula 'en Christo'. Paul, especially, uses it with great frequency and in a variety of contexts to stress the intimate union of believers with Christ. He refers to 'speaking' in Christ (Rom. 9:1), to his 'handiwork' in the Lord, to 'joy in the Lord' (Phil. 3:1), to 'the way of life in Christ' (1 Cor. 4:17) and, comprehensively, to being 'united with Christ Jesus' (Rom. 8:1) and to 'life . . . . in Christ Jesus' (2 Tim. 1:1). These varied uses of the term 'in Christ' reflect a vital element in the New Testament view of salvation, namely, the impossibility in the last analysis of separating Christ from our life in faith, from our salvation. Our life is 'hidden in Christ with God'; Christ 'is our life' (Col. 3:3). The essential core of our salvation, our Christian identity, has been given us 'en Christo'.

This phrase has a cultural background, of course.

Did the use of it by Christians mean a Hellenization of their faith? I think not. The use of this term in the life of the Church and in Christian theology did not amount to an infiltration of Hellenistic mysticism. What was being taken up here, on the contrary, was the messianic heritage of the Old Testament. The title 'Christos' was being used in its quite concrete Old Testament sense. This is also important for the light it sheds on the New Testament view of salvation. As the variety of terms used with the 'en Christo' formula impressively demonstrates, salvation in Christ embraces not just the realms of the spirit, the soul, the beyond, but the entire Christian life, leaving its imprint on all our words and deeds. According to the New Testament, our human life 'in Christ' is shifted out of a context of sheer blind factitiousness and fatality, is no longer at the mercy of chance circumstances and processes, but is set within the horizon of an eschatological hope which already here and now upholds us and transforms us, in the direction of the renewal of our hearts and our circumstances.

We now turn to the other—first—name of the central New Testament figure: *Jesus*. Here we descend from the lofty heights of the messianic tradition to the unmistakably ordinary everyday level of the Jewish context and in doing so come to another aspect of 'salvation from the Jews'. The name 'Jesus' was a common one already in Old Testament times and even in Jesus' own day. 'Jesus' is the Greek equivalent of the Hebrew name *'Jehoshua'*. A whole series of Old Testament characters bore this name, the most outstanding of them being undoubtedly 'Joshua the son of Nun', Israel's leader at the time of the Exodus, and Joshua the High Priest, the son of Jehozadak, who accompanied Zerubbabel on the return from Exile. The name continued to be a popular one in the Jewish world right down to the beginning of the second century A.D. Three of the seventy-two translators of the Septuagint bore the already Graecized name 'Jesus'. We find a similar situation in the New Testament where others beside Jesus of Nazareth were also called 'Jesus'.

Faced with these facts, it might seem contrived and unconvincing to press this quite ordinary name to furnish a contribution to our understanding of the New Testament view of salvation. Yet the most obvious feature of this name, its outer ordinariness, is of the very greatest importance. What comes to expression in this name, with all its cultural and religious associations, is the *unqualified humanity of the Saviour and*, with it, the concrete historicity of salvation. Far from being something essentially mythological or metaphysical, the salvation to which Christians bear witness is essentially historical; part and parcel of *salvation* history, certainly, but for that precise reason, essentially *historical*. In *this* historical person, bearing *this* ordinary common-place human name, the Christ, the Son of God, the Lord, has appeared. Indeed, the person known under these majestic titles is identical with, is none other than, this historical human being, Jesus of Nazareth.

Here is the difference between the apostles and the Gnostics: 'There is no separation between an earthly body and a Christ who put on this body, as in Christian Gnosticism. *Jesous* is *ho Kurios,* and not something apart from him. Hence the Gospels, the missionary preaching of Acts and Paul (Gal. 3:1) present this Jesus of Nazareth and say that God has made this man the Lord and the Judge: *en andri ho horizen* 'by a man of his choosing' Acts 17:31'.[21]

Having said just now that the *en Christo* is at the very heart of the Christian faith, we are now justified in adding—since both names are inseparably connected by the New Testament—that this particular name, the historical human being it quite specifically designates, Jesus the Christ, is at the very heart of the Christian faith. Salvation has contingent historical contours, those of this particular human life, and this is important not only from a doctrinal but also and above all from an ethical standpoint. This being the case, the vision and the practice of salvation cannot be something arbitrary, for which different symbols could equally well serve. 'Christ' is not just a code name for our own or some general human self-understanding which we are free to fill in as we please. Christ is Jesus. The way of salvation is to be understood and its binding ethical obligations practiced in strict accordance with his life and teachings. The direction and way for our discipleship is given in and with the name Jesus. Here, I believe, is the soteriological importance of this simple name, Jesus of Nazareth.

But there is still another essential aspect. According to the testimony of the gospels, this very ordinary name 'Jesus' takes on a very specific and pregnant meaning in the case of this particular bearer of it. Let me remind you of my general remarks about the significance of names in the biblical world earlier in this section: names here are not just meaningless sounds—'sounds and fury, signifying nothing'—but can take on prophetic significance. And in the case of Jesus this is precisely what happens. 'According to Mt. and Lk. the name *Jeshua = Jesous* is not accidental. It is given to the child of Mary by virtue of the divine promise. Mt. 1:21 explains this as follows: 'You shall give him the name Jesus (Saviour), for he will save his people from their sins'.[22]

In our present context there are at least three good reasons why we should recall this theological affirmation in the prologue to Matthew's gospel, the purpose of which is to provide a pregnant theological summary indicating in advance the content of the ensuing Christian account of Jesus of Nazareth.

a)   The name of the man from Nazareth is taken literally, at its face value: the name 'Jesus' is the *programme* he is to carry out. His name means: *Yahweh is the Saviour,* and this, as I have already pointed out, is one of the main confessions of Israel's faith. In other words, despite the utterly contingent character of raw human history, what begins in this human being is a part — or, more accurately, the centre — of the history of salvation. The seal is now finally set on the covenant of salvation established, but also constantly called in question, in the Old Testament. This is the 'meaning' and 'purpose' of the history inseparably connected with Jesus — from the very outset.

• b)   In this history, in the history of salvation, what is at stake is the deliverance of God's people, the deliverance of the peoples. This gives the salvation made accessible in the life of Jesus its distinctive profile. What is at stake here is human deliverance, human *liberation.* Without wishing to attach too much weight to it, the possible allusion here to the Joshua of the Old Testament may · perhaps be theologically significant. The New Testament Joshua-Jesus completes the ministry of the Old Testament Joshua. In the name of Jesus, the new and final Exodus of God's people from the 'houses of bondage' in the far country of our alienation is begun and completed. Salvation is therefore to be understood in the context of the history of liberation.

c)   This history of liberation is, of course, the history of an historical deliverance, of an Exodus to

54

a greater justice and freedom in an earthly, individual and social sense. But this liberation points beyond itself, transcends every earthly or social plane. The aim is not just to make relative improvements possible but to overcome 'radical evil', something which cannot be accomplished by any act of liberation or social achievement in history. This is referred to in Matthew when he comments on the explanation of Jesus' name: ' . . . . because he will *save* his people *from their sins'*. J. Schniewind writes as follows in his commentary: 'In both the Old Testament and the New, the forgiveness of sins is a term which summarises God's salvation in its entirety. It means far more than the cancellation of specific evil deeds; it means the abolition of the divorce between God and humankind'.[23] Salvation in the name of Jesus Christ means precisely that: the abolition of the divorce, liberation in reconciliation.

Prophet, Priest, King: Problems Involved in the Doctrine of the Threefold Office

Pursuing our attempt to define the 'centre of salvation', we turn from the 'name' of Jesus Christ to his 'saving work'. To tackle this theme, I shall make use of the doctrine of Christ's Three Offices. This is the doctrine in which traditional dogmatics — both Protestant and Catholic — has often dealt with the person and work of Christ, i.e. with soteriology.

The terminology used in this presentation of the theme has little to attract us today. 'Office' strongly suggests officialdom and even rank bureaucracy, and these are hardly inviting prospects for anyone today. It is also an undeniable fact that this traditional treatment of salvation in Christ has been dogged by certain bureaucratic tendencies. It has all too easily allowed the organic and dynamic life work of Jesus Christ to be divided up, sometimes almost pedantically, into various pigeon-holes. These might vary in number: at first the ancient Church recognized only two offices of Christ (*munus* or *officium duplex*), namely, the office of priest and the office of king. Christian thinking in the field of soteriology was largely dominated by these two categories down to the time of the Reformation. A third office, that of prophet, the *munus prophet-icum,* did sometimes come into the reckoning but it was left to Calvin to present and develop the full potentialities of a 'threefold' pattern for the first time, in his *Geneva Catechism.* Subsequently this pattern largely held the field. Even today the *munus triplex* still plays an important role in doctrinal thought—even in Catholic dogmatics.

The most rebarbative feature of this pattern is its use of the term 'office' but also the ease with which 'the sacred number three' could transform the doctrine into an 'embellishment, a sacred dogmatic game' (Otto Weber).[24] Our modern discomfort with the term 'office', natural as it is, should not, however, blind us to the doctrinal purpose this doctrine was meant to serve. There are positive points about the doctrine of the threefold office of Christ, and I would like to point out two of them, at least. The purpose of the term *officium* or *munus* is, in the first place, to 'bring the work of Jesus out of the purely private, arbitrary, accidental realm' (Otto Weber).[25] Christ's work of salvation is *no private affair,* no autocratic achievement of some Promethean notability. It is a 'work' entrusted to him and undertaken by him, a work completed by him on behalf of his fellow human-beings. It is not merely 'his business' but the work of the mediator, 'the business between God and humanity', or, more precisely, God's saving work on behalf of human-kind. The term 'office' points to this dimension of the work of Jesus Christ. And this reference justifies the use of the term even if nowadays we prefer to avoid it and look for a different terminology, for example, the term 'mission' in the sense of the *missio Dei*. We are still bound to respect the intention.

There is another point in favour of the doctrine of the threefold office: it counteracts any tendency to restrict redemption or to interpret it one-sidedly, i.e. any *one-dimensional* view of salvation. We find this tendency represented throughout the entire course of doctrinal history. For example, the prophetic element in the ministry of Jesus was exaggerated, Jesus being seen primarily as the 'Great Teacher' and his work primarily as revelation and enlightenment. A Gnostic or rationalist over-simplification of the work of salvation was the danger here. Or, again, the priestly role of Christ could be over-emphasized, the *beneficia* of his forgiveness and reconciliation, at the risk of putting all the weight on the 'inner aspects' of salvation and its passive reception. When Christianity followed this way it settled down as an individualistic 'religion of redemption'. A further temptation was to stress the kingly authority of Jesus Christ and to make this the distinctive and even unique aspect of his salvation, thereby encouraging a tendency to a theocratic or even an ecclesiocratic view of the world.

The doctrine of the threefold office of Christ, by reminding us of the reality and mutual solidarity of all three dimensions in the work of Christ, resists these one-sided tendencies. A clear distinction is made between the three 'offices' but they are also held together and, above all, related to each other. This prevents us from any isolation and abstract interpretation of the different dimensions of salvation. The doctrine of the three offices of Christ has an important critical and methodological role to play in both soteriology and christology. This is why we are concerned with it in this chapter, though, I repeat, with no notion of treating its terms as sacrosanct.

Let us now look at the doctrine of the three offices in more detail. It is not found as such in the Bible itself but is the fruit of the Church's reflection on doctrine. Yet this church explanation does not lack a biblical anchorage or at least a biblical impetus. It is an attempt to bring out the meaning of the title 'Christos' and of the work of Jesus Christ. The Old Testament background is in itself sufficient to warrant such an attempt. The 'messiah' is the 'anointed one'. But basically there are three kinds of 'anointed ones' in the Old Testament: kings, priests and prophets. Confronted with Christ's life and work, the disciples saw in them the fulfilment of the messianic hope and this became the centre of their message. What more natural, then, than that Christian theologians should develop their soteriology in precisely these three directions and speak of the prophetic, priestly and royal role and work of Jesus Christ? Particular biblical themes were accordingly picked up and elaborated very freely in the light of the total person and work of Christ. The underlying concern was to develop the main dimensions of salvation as they understood it, differentiating between these dimensions but seeing them at the same time in their indissoluble unity and interaction. The following notes on the doctrine of Christ's three offices have a similar purpose.

1. There is a certain ambiguity in the New Testament references to Jesus of Nazareth as a *prophet*. Some features of his teaching and way of life, of course, led people around him to interpret

him in terms of current ideas about prophecy. Jesus himself, however, did not do so. Indeed there is clear evidence that he opposed any such identification of himself with the prophets. The characteristic prophetic assertion 'Thus saith the Lord!' is not employed by Jesus. The words he does use, 'But I say to you . . . . ' would have been inconceivable on the lips of the prophets. The reports of the New Testament witnesses make it very clear that the person encountered here was more than a prophet. The prophetic intensity which characterizes, for example, Mohammed's sense of vocation is quite foreign to the New Testament.

In the New Testament presentation of the work of Jesus, however, there is unquestionably a prophetic dimension with messianic and eschatological overtones. By this latter qualification I mean that, although traditional categories are quite insufficient to warrant the description of Jesus as a prophet, he is nevertheless undoubtedly the heir to prophetic promises and is in this sense the one who in the history of salvation fulfils the prophetic office. He is the revealer, the witness; he brings, indeed he embodies, the truth. The significance of this for us is that redemption in Christ is no blind inexpressible mystery but the establishment of salvation articulated as word and truth. His salvation contains, indeed is, *instruction*.

This 'office' of Jesus is seldom illustrated as vividly and as clearly as it is in the Lukan version of *Jesus' first sermon* (Lk. 4:41-21). This synoptic passage looms large in contemporary ecumenical theology. It is occasionally referred to as 'the Nazareth Manifesto'! And it is indeed a key passage for the understanding of Jesus' view of salvation. In our present context it is significant in at least three respects:

(a)   It defines quite unambiguously the *frame of reference,* the *background* of the prophetic office. Jesus' instruction is framed in a salvation-history, an eschatological, indeed specifically messianic setting. The heart of the Lukan passage, significantly enough, is a fundamental Old Testament statement of biblical hope for the future. The Isaianic 'Good news of the coming salvation' is proclaimed. In the synagogue of his home town, Jesus chooses this messianic promise as his text and then gives his own interpretation of it. This interpretation is only a single sentence—but what a sentence! Jesus' first instruction is this: 'Today in your very hearing this text has come true'. This is nothing less than a messianic proclamation of the presence of the eschatological salvation. The messianic future has begun! With the coming of Jesus, God Himself is taking charge of His people with final authority and right.

This frame of reference is of fundamental importance if we are rightly to understand Jesus' prophetic role and work. It qualifies and defines all Jesus' words and works from start to finish. The other evangelists represent Jesus as beginning with an even more compressed message: 'The time has come; the kingdom of God is upon you; repent, and believe the Gospel' (Mk. 1:15). The words differ but the message remains the same. The world finds itself brought close to God in His liberating presence. The religious music of the future becomes an all-transforming change in the present. Two terms, faith and repentance, are used to describe this transformation. Both these terms affirm that history is not 'a tale told by an idiot'. There is more to reality than the circumstances which shape us, the conditions which imprison us. Whenever anyone commits himself to Jesus, believes in his kingdom, turns round and follows him, these circumstances and conditions are broken open, demythologized, and set moving.

Here is the horizon, indeed, the fundamental instruction of the prophecy of Jesus: it is a question of recognizing the signs of the times, of not letting *our* 'today' slip thoughtlessly and aimlessly through our fingers but letting it be renewed and shaped by the completeness of *his* 'today'. Because God is 'at hand', new life is possible for all, and it is meant to be and should be lived, therefore. Our last opportunity should not, need not, be wasted. 'Faith' and 'conversion' are the order of the day, therefore, not as law but as Gospel. This is the radical instruction of Jesus.

(b) This main instruction is also translated into more specific directives. Isaiah's messianic promises become, in fact, signposts of the coming kingdom of God. The clear outlines of the prophetic mission of Jesus emerge: 'He has sent me to announce good news to the poor, to proclaim release for prisoners and recovery of sight for the blind; to let the broken victims go free' (Lk. 4:18f.). The most important areas of life or, more specifically, the key situations of human distress and need are lined in with clear strokes. They cover a wide range of human situations. Both in the Old Testament promise and in its New Testament fulfilment, the focus is on spiritual, material, political and social distress, both individual and collective. In principle, no distress of any kind is excluded from the mission of Jesus. That was far from being an obvious position. How often have we been offered portraits of the 'saviour' and ideas of 'mission' which almost completely ignore whole areas of human life and lead (mis-lead) people either into religious idealism or political materialism! From the very outset, Jesus rules out all doctrinaire stereotypes of his prophetic office.

Following the line of Old Testament prophecy, moreover, the mission of Jesus has a clear and unambiguous bias: it is directed primarily to the 'poor', in the inclusive Old Testament sense of this term, i.e. embracing both the materially poor and the religiously poor. Jesus identifies himself with the lowly, the outcasts, all who are despised and discriminated against. No honest exegesis can excise this feature from the gospels. We have here an authentic and constant instruction of Jesus. The Gospel requires us to be partisan. Not in any ideological or party-political sense, of course. Jesus does not make himself the focal point of a 'popular front' or recruit men and women for the class war. We are surprised and pleased when we note that he counts on an audience for his 'Good News' even on the other side of the social or religious barriers! He does not set up new laws in opposition to the old. Even for the 'other side' at any given moment, his Gospel remains a message of hope, though at the same time an explicit, authoritative, challenging promise, too. It is a summons to genuine *metanoia*, to real repentance and conversion. The joyful feast which Jesus is able to attend even in the house of the wealthy and deeply compromised collaborator Zacchaeus is more than just a banquet, it is a celebration of repentance and conversion.

(c) What is the *goal* of the prophetic mission of Jesus Christ? A significant clue to the answer to this question is provided by the Lukan passage, occurring moreover in the concluding summary of the Isaiah quotation. Here Jesus picks up the Old Testament theme of 'the year of the Lord's favour'. This is a reference to the Jubilee Year which was supposed to be celebrated in Israel every fiftieth year. This institution had important social implications: all Israelites who had come a cropper economically or politically in the previous period were to be set free. The Jubilee Year was also a sign of God's drawing near to His people. This year of freedom, this year of grace, was 'the acceptable year of the Lord', 'the year of the Lord's favour'.

It is obviously along these lines that Jesus understood his mission. The *kingdom of God* which Jesus proclaimed was concerned with freedom and justice, but also and above all with love and grace. As I understand it, these four concepts point to the central emphases of the prophecy of Jesus. Among them, *grace* has a preeminent place. It is worthy of notice that Jesus leaves the quotation from Isaiah incomplete. The phrase 'the day of vengeance of our God' (Isaiah 61:2) is omitted. In other words, instead of the prophetic 'Yes and No' we have the evangelical 'Yes'. It is to this emphasis in the life and ministry of Jesus that Paul is referring when he speaks of that life and ministry and declares: 'The Son of God, Christ Jesus . . . . was never a blend of Yes and No. With him it was, and is, Yes. He is the Yes pronounced upon God's promises, every one of them' (2 Cor. 1:20 NEB). In his words, deeds and sufferings, Jesus bore witness to this Yes of God to humankind. This is his prophetic instruction: amid the mercilessness of our human world and its movements, we are never to allow his mercy and grace to be forgotten.

2. This mention of the grace of our Lord Jesus Christ brings us at once to the second set of questions in soteriology, usually dealt with in connection with Christ's *priestly office*. Truth and grace are intimately connected. 'Grace and truth came

through Jesus Christ', we read in the Johannine summary of Jesus' work. And 'out of his full store we have all received grace upon grace' (Jn. 1:16f.). The instruction given in Jesus is no law, nor is his truth merely 'disclosure'. His instruction brings healing, his truth salvation. He is not only prophet and king but also mediator, reconciler, priest.

This 'office' of Jesus is explicitly developed and emphasized in the New Testament, most clearly in the *Epistle to the Hebrews*. This letter provides us with a detailed argument interpreting the office of Christ dialectically in the light of the Old Testament priesthood. The great task of the priests of the Old Testament, i.e. as witnesses of forgiveness, ministers of reconciliation, mediators of the covenant, making salvation a present reality to God's people, is assumed and fulfilled by Christ. In contrast to the significant but defective Levitical priesthood, Christ is 'a priest for ever, in the succession of Melchizedek' (Heb. 7:17, cf. 7:21). His sacrifice is no mere provisional sign of salvation requiring constant repetition but the unique, once-for-all eschatological work of salvation. 'The blood of his sacrifice is his own blood, not the blood of goats and calves; and thus he has entered the sanctuary once and for all and secured an eternal deliverance' (9:12). He is therefore 'the mediator of a new covenant' (9:15), the one who has finally overcome the alienation between God and humankind. He is God stepping into the breach caused by sin, the sin which imperils and destroys God's creation. He is the one who really establishes reconciliation. This is what the *Epistle to the Hebrews* means when it declares enthusiastically: 'Just such a priest we have, and he has taken his seat at the right hand of the throne of Majesty in the heavens, a ministrant in the real sanctuary, the tent pitched by the Lord and not by man' (Heb. 8:2).

This sounds triumphalistic yet 'triumphalistic' is the very last epithet which can reasonably be applied to the context in which this priestly office of Jesus is fulfilled: the context of death on the cross, the sufferings of Jesus in solidarity with sinful humanity. It should not be overlooked that the author's whole argument for the superiority of Jesus' priesthood rests precisely on this fact, not on the basis of some outstanding Promethean achievement but on that of his pioneering obedience even unto death. 'For ours is not a high priest unable to sympathize with our weakness, but one who, because of his likeness to us, has been tested in every way, only without sin' (4:15 NEB). Precisely here, according to the *Epistle to the Hebrews,* our salvation lies: because our God is the God who acts and suffers with Jesus in his life, we have not been abandoned to ourselves in the midst of our human life with all our weakness and estrangement, we are no longer at the mercy of the annihilating abyss. From God's side, a lifeline, a bridge, is thrown across to each one of us in our personal need and distress. For our sakes someone took his journey to the very limits of this far country of sin and death, established and sealed there the covenant of eternal fidelity, keeps and upholds it: namely, Jesus the priest.

This view of the 'office of Christ' is not peculiar to *Hebrews.* Although we seldom find the theme and the terminology occurring elsewhere in the New Testament with the same density as in *Hebrews,* this view of Christ's work faithfully reflects the basic conception of the New Testament. Christ's priestly sacrifice is emphasized in the whole of the New Testament, even if the terms and the contexts differ and the emphasis varies from place to place. The essential point at stake here is the saving significance of the cross and death of Jesus. And the cross is right at the centre of the New Testament. The apostles desired to testify to 'nothing but Jesus Christ — Christ nailed to the cross' (1 Cor. 2:2).

Nor was this true only of the apostles. Even Jesus himself appears to have felt that the theme of suffering and death was of vital importance, unmistakably so in connection precisely with his 'office', his 'missio Dei', to judge by the way the synoptic gospels present him as constantly wrestling to understand and carry out this mission and persisting in obedience to it even in his sufferings and death. A great number of New Testament passages could be cited in support of this. While they may not always provide the *ipsissima verba* of Jesus (which in any case are hard to establish with any certainty), they certainly reflect his *ipsissima intentio*. And this 'deepest intention' as reflected in the gospels clearly points in this priestly direction: 'he (the Son of Man) did not come to be served, but to serve, and to give up his life as a ransom for many' (Mt. 20:28). This devoted concern for the neighbour, this unqualified love for his fellow human beings, is clearly the *cantus firmus* of the polyphonic life of Jesus, and not just of his active life but very definitely of his 'passive' life as well, not just in his actions but intensely in his sufferings, in his cross and death, too. Profoundly shaken though the disciples were by the death of Jesus, they were nevertheless able, therefore, to continue this fundamental dimension of his ministry in their own apostolic preaching and in that of the early Church.

The keys for interpreting the sufferings and death of Jesus were provided by certain Old Testament themes: for example, the idea of the sin-offering, of vicarious suffering, of the eschatological redemption of the debtor, of the passover meal. A specially important role is played by the witness of

Second Isaiah to the suffering servant of God. The fate of Jesus seemed to be predicted here right down to the very details: 'He had no beauty, no majesty to draw our eyes, ... we despised him, we held him of no account . . . . Yet on himself he bore our sufferings, our torments he endured . . . . but he was pierced for our transgressions, tortured for our iniquities; the chastisement he bore is health for us and by his scourging we are healed . . . . he was stricken to the death for my people's transgression. He was assigned a grave with the wicked, a burial place among the refuse of mankind, though he had done no violence and spoken no word of treachery . . . . ' (Isaiah 53, NEB).

The "song of the suffering servant" 'is used in the very early creed in 1 Cor. 15:3-5, and in the early tradition of the Last Supper (1 Cor. 11:24; Mk. 14: 24 par.) to interpret the death of Jesus as a represent-ative expiatory death for the salvation of men. Subsequently this interpretation became funda-mental to the Christian understanding of the Redemption in general and the Eucharist in particular' (Kasper).[26]

This fundamental biblical view of the priestly office of Jesus Christ set Christian theology, i.e. soteriology, its most important task, namely, the development of the various themes suggested but by no means systematically presented by the Old and New Testaments, within the context of Christian dogmatics. Christian dogmatics has been engaged in this task throughout church history and some of the conceptions which emerged as a result will be looked at in detail in the next chapter on 'Salvation as Reconciliation'. All I want to say at this point is that the elaboration of the *munus sacerdotale* constitutes one of the traditional tasks of Christian theology.

3. The kingly office, the *munus regium* of Christ, has received less attention in the history of doctrine than the priestly office. In view of the central place of the kingdom of God theme in the message of Jesus and the undeniable place of the message of 'Christ's kingship' in the apostolic preaching, this neglect seems astonishing. The words 'King of the Jews' were even placed over the cross of Jesus, while the shortest creed used in the early Church to sum up the experience and message of his resurrection is 'Jesus is Lord'. It is an encouraging sign, therefore, that this theme in particular (and with it the royal office of Christ) should have come to the forefront in recent ecumenical theology.[27]

We should harbour no illusions: the idea of the 'kingly office' is wide open to misunderstanding, and this makes it all the more necessary to be precise as to its theological significance. A. Ritschl warned us a century ago: 'Unless the concept of his (Christ's) present kingship can be given substance by the specific features of his historic ministry, it is either a worthless metaphor or an open invitation to fanaticism of every sort'.[28] We still need this warning today. But it is not just our contemporaries, for whom the term 'royal sovereignty' suggests an authoritarianism which is suspect in a democratic age, who need this warning. Explanations are also called for in respect of the legacy of church history. How often christocratic ideas have been taken to imply totalitarian theocratic and even ecclesiocratic programmes! And how often the Church has adopted a policy whereby a culture and a society has been regimented under the banner of 'Christ the King!' More often than not the New Testament background of Christ's 'kingship' has been swept aside and even distorted by such attitudes. Christ's kingship, according to the New Testament, is rooted in the actual history of Jesus of Nazareth, as this is reflected, for example, in Phil. 2:5-11, the *locus classicus* of the Pauline view of kingship. It is essential to keep this foundation in mind, otherwise the idea of kingship leads to misunderstandings due to the loaded sociological and ideological presuppositions about kingship in the oriental, Hellenistic (and later in the medieval) world. Kingship is then almost inevitably interpreted as domination, power, magical authority, absolute despotism, and so on, and the way cleared for a political abuse of the theological concept of 'royal authority'. Biblically interpreted, however, Christ's kingship is no magic absolute almightiness. It is not 'the control of inert or resistant objects in virtue of greater force' (E. Schweizer),[29] but the (personal) power of redemptive sacrifice, service, philanthropy (Tit. 3:4) and reconciliation. The Lord rules, not as a despot but by his love and voluntary service. Conversely—and this has critical implications for society—the real lord is not the tyrant bristling with power, the real lord is the serving man from Nazareth. The power of salvation and not salvation through power is his way and his work.

When we insist on Christ's 'kingship', his 'royal office', we are stressing this genuine 'power of salvation', the real authority of Jesus, and therefore *the inescapable consequences of salvation*. Salvation does not merely bring enlightenment, it does not only guarantee the forgiveness of sins and redemption through the sacrifice of the Son of God; at the same time it draws us irrevocably into discipleship, into the movement of obedience to the royal word of Jesus. In the *munus regium*, therefore, the *ethical dimension* of soteriology comes into the centre of the stage. We are not to confuse this ethical dimension with moralism of any kind. What the vision of

Christ's kingship and glory discloses primarily is the vista of liberation, the sight of the Risen Lord who 'has burst all bonds' and whose Spirit is accordingly the Spirit of liberty. The ethics of salvation is not a legalistic ethic of achievement but the ethics of discipleship. 'The rod or sceptre of his kingdom is the Gospel', as Luther properly insisted.[30]

Yet this 'rod or sceptre' points to the binding way of this freedom. Jesus the King expects us to take his way of life seriously. It is impossible to enjoy his salvation without at the same time being invited and required to conform to it and to live accordingly. The Gospel indicative cannot be divorced from its imperative — and *vice versa*. This is made quite clear in the example of the apostles, including the formal structure of their letters.

We have to differentiate between (but not separate) *two stages* or two forms of this kingship of Christ: the Church and the world (traditional language spoke somewhat questionably here of 'two kingdoms'). The realm of Christ's royal office has a definite structure. He is not sovereign merely in a general sense; his sovereignty primarily means *the Church* and it is understood and attested in faith. New Testament scholarship properly points out that the original form of the Christian creed was one in which Christ was confessed primarily as Lord of the Church. 'Come, Lord Jesus!' is undoubtedly the oldest prayer of the Church, going back to the time when it was still prayed in Aramaic. In this connection the image of the 'body of Christ' is particularly important, since it certainly refers to the Church and not to the world in general. The life of the Christian community, the Church, is the concrete context of Christ's kingly rule. Here we have the inescapable first stage of the *munus regium,* its primary form.

But the second follows hard on the first. Although the biblical vision of Christ's kingship has a pneumatological and ecclesiological basis, it undoubtedly at the same time reaches further than the area of the Church. The Lord of the Church is 'supreme over every spiritual ruler and authority' (Col. 2:10 GNB). He is the *Lord of the world.* Even if the cosmological approach is false, the cosmological horizon of the royal office of Christ is indispensable. At any rate this is the direction in which the statements of the New Testament logically point. Anchored in ecclesiology, they have a dynamic thrust outwards towards the world. When the Christian community confesses 'Jesus is Lord' (*kurios Jesous*) — as the Hellenistic community in particular actually did in face of the especially intense fear of the forces of fate and destiny displayed by the people around it — the encouragement received by the Christian community is not just of a private kind; it experiences the eschatological deliverance. All other powers are here dethroned, at least in the sense that their claim to be finally decisive is denied. This clears the decks for a clear view of the whole creation in its universal range. Indeed, for more than a clear view of it. The way now leads the Christian community out on its mission 'into all the world'. Christ's royal office, the kingdom of God, concerns 'all the world'; witness to it cannot stop at the frontiers of the Church. Christianity from the very beginning has known itself to be the movement of 'public salvation' and not merely a private religion.

I pointed out earlier the importance of distinguishing between but not separating the two forms of the royal office of Jesus. Church history affords us all too many illustrations of the dangers of ignoring this dictum. Failure to distinguish

71

between the believing community and secular society as the two realms of Christ's kingship, leads to the fanaticism of theocratic panaceas, the subordination of the world to tutelage or else to its sacralization, or to making the Gospel into a law. Lutheran theology in particular has protested vigorously against such an abuse of Christ's royal office either by clericalism or by fanaticism. In his reflections on the *munus regium* in his *Institutio,* Calvin's chief concern is to warn against false secular applications of this doctrine. There is also a temptation, however, in the opposite direction. While it may not be as obvious as the other temptation, it is in my view a much more dangerous one because it has in fact been a constant incubus in church history. I mean the *false separation* of the two realms, or in other words a form of the 'two kingdom doctrine' which fails to venture the second step but which, when it reaches the frontiers of the Christian community, ceases to confess Christ's kingship with all its consequences for the transformation of the world; which so emphasizes the 'not yet' of the biblical vision of the kingdom of God that it obscures and even loses sight altogether of the ethically so important accompanying dialectical New Testament 'now already' of that kingdom; which acts as if the 'sceptre' and 'rod' of the Gospel has no authority in the secular world. The temptation here is to come to terms with the world, to adapt to it, adopting a supposedly 'realistic' but in reality fainthearted and faithless attitude — *etsi Deus (etsi Christus) non daretur!* — as if there were no God and no Christ! As I see it, real witness to Christ's kingship takes place when the pneumatological reality of that kingship is accepted in faith, when, along with this and in full recognition of the eschatological 'not yet', there is already a sober reckoning with reconciliation and liberation and already a real attempt to act for reconciliation and liberation in accordance with and in the direction indicated by the 'specific features' of that pneumatological reality. The centre of salvation confronts us in the very midst of our life.

3

Salvation as Reconciliation

The Narrow Gate of Redemption

'The heart of the Christian message is the message of reconciliation', declares W. Joest in his article on 'Reconciliation' in an important German dictionary of religion.[31] One of the main soteriological statements in the New Testament is that 'God was in Christ reconciling the world to himself, no longer holding men's misdeeds against them' (2 Cor. 5:19). From the biblical standpoint, of course, salvation cannot be reduced simply to the cancellation of sin and guilt. It also includes rebirth, sanctification, the new creation. The event of our reconciliation is, however, the foundation of salvation. 'Not to understand salvation as, in the last analysis, reconciliation, would be to misunderstand it, either eudaemonistically, as protection against evil and the gift or promise of earthly riches, or moralistically, as simply instruction in a purified form of religion and morality' (Joest).[32]

This emphasis on reconciliation in the Christian view of salvation is far from self-evident. Certainly it has the support of some important figures in recent theological history: A. Ritschl and M. Kähler, for example, and more recently and outstandingly, Karl Barth. The Swiss theologian presents his christology — which he develops in inseparable connection with his soteriology — under the title: 'The Doctrine of Reconciliation'. But even so loyal a student of Barth as Otto Weber points out the problems arising from this emphasis on reconciliation in the context of soteriology. Broadly speaking, there is a 'tacit consensus in the history of doctrine until now' which opposes Barth, Ritschl and Kähler on this point.[33] The doctrine of reconciliation has only a relatively narrow basis in the New Testament and in church history. It would be a dubious restriction of soteriology if we were to reduce the message of salvation to the theme of reconciliation (though this is certainly not the intention either of Joest in the statements just quoted or of Barth in his *Church Dogmatics*).

I take Weber's warning — and that of the mainstream of doctrinal history — very seriously. The very title of my book — 'Reconciliation *and* Liberation' — indicates my concern to repudiate all attempts to simplify by reduction. Salvation is both reconciliation and liberation. It is not my intention here to play two diametrically opposed themes off against each other. In the biblical view, reconciliation and liberation are intimately interrelated. But by deliberately choosing to develop the theme of 'the work of Christ' in two separate chapters, I wish to make it clear even by the formal arrangement of the material that 'salvation in Christ' can never be grasped in a *single* train of argument, in a *single* range of ideas. The 'multi-dimensional' character of salvation must be respected both in dogmatics and in ethics.

That being said, Joest's dictum and Barth's approach in his *Church Dogmatics* still seem to me to make sense: the term 'reconciliation' goes to the very heart of the New Testament message of salvation. Quantitatively, in terms of the frequency of its appearance, this term may have a relatively narrow New Testament basis, but qualitatively, measured by its substance, weight and importance, it does indeed constitute the heart of the message and theology of the New Testament. We can only agree with Barth when, at a vital point in the development of his doctrine of reconciliation, he asserts that 'all theology depends' on the fact that 'the Judge was judged in our place'. The same is true of his final conclusion: 'There is no avoiding this strait gate'[34] — provided we remember that the way of faith does not end at this 'strait gate' but leads through it and beyond, and that salvation as reconciliation is at the same time to be understood and practiced as liberation in the widest sense.

A brief glance now at the 'narrow basis' of the concept of reconciliation in the New Testament. In the New Testament *katalassein* and *katallage* are exclusively Pauline terms. Only in the important 'Sermon on the Mount' do we find a related term used elsewhere in the New Testament. The reference here is to 'reconciliation with the brother' (Mt. 5:24), i.e. to human relationships, just as Paul also refers to reconciliation between husband and wife (in 1 Cor. 7:11, for example). We must not lose sight of this concrete use of the term in the area of relationships between persons for it links up with the important ethical dimension of reconciliation to which we shall have to return later. But in its doctrinal application, which is the commonest in Paul, *katalassein* refers to what happens in the relationship between God and humanity and between God and the world. Let us now consider some of the most important features of the term 'reconciliation' and the event to which it refers.

1.   The New Testament is unhesitant and quite clear as to who the *subject* or agent of reconciliation is. Only two names come into the picture here: God and Christ, God in Christ. The grammatical evidence points in the same direction: *katalassein* (to reconcile) is used only of God, *katallagenai* (to be reconciled) only of humanity. The key statement of 2 Cor. 5:18f. has already been quoted: God reconciles the world with himself. In other words: 'He is not reconciled. Nor does he reconcile himself to us or to the world. On the contrary, we are reconciled to God (Rom. 5:10) or reconcile ourselves to him (2 Cor. 5:20). Thus God and man are not on equal terms in relation to reconciliation. Reconciliation is not reciprocal in the sense that both equally become friends where they were enemies. The supremacy of God over man is maintained in every respect!'[35] We shall have to keep this content of the apostolic view of reconciliation in mind when we come to examine and weigh critically the development of soteriology in the history of the Church.

2.   That God in Christ is the only subject or agent of reconciliation does not mean that human beings are turned into mere *objects*. The 'subject-object' formula is as little help in interpreting the event of reconciliation as it is in other theological problems. In the history of the Church the problem has sometimes been put in the form of the question: Do human beings share actively or passively in the event of reconciliation? In the article already quoted, Büchsel provides a lapidary answer to this question: 'They (human beings) are made active. By the *diakonia tes katallages* (the service of reconciliation), which brings God's deed of love near to them, God makes them active, gives them the right and the ability to be reconciled with God . . . . We have

received reconciliation (Rom. 5:11) but definitely not in the way we received blows but in such a way that God has invited us (2 Cor. 5:20) . . . . The fact that Paul describes the word of reconciliation as a request, completely excludes the possibility that he thought of our being and behaving merely passively in reconciliation'.[36]

3.   The mobilizing effect of the event of reconciliation is also shown by the comprehensive attestation of the concept in the New Testament, by the fact that it is *cross-concerned* with other central concepts as justification, justice and newness of life. Rudolf Bultmann draws attention to this in his *Theology of the New Testament*: 'Another term can be substituted for the term "righteousness" (or the cognate verb) as the designation of the new situation which God Himself has opened up to man: "reconciliation" (or the cognate verb —*katallage* and *katallagenai*). Examination of Paul's statements on "righteousness" and those on "reconciliation" results in mutual corroboration'.[37] In the light of the New Testament witness, therefore, reconciliation cannot possibly be interpreted in a purely private or passive sense. Far more is involved than the transformation of our inner world and attitudes. Established in Christ, reconciliation points to a very real change in 'God's world', too, and since it is the event which embodies God's justice it also demands a correspondingly real change in our human world as well.

4.   This change in God's world and in our human world cannot be regarded as something arbitrary or optional. Its outlines are clearly indicated in the New Testament. So far as divine-human relationships are concerned, reconciliation primarily means the end of the *enmity* between God and us. The

most impressive statement of this change is found in Rom. 5:10. We who were 'God's enemies' have been reconciled with God. Between us and God yawned the gaping chasm of sin (2 Cor. 5:19; Rom. 5:15ff. Cf. also Eph. 1:7; 2:1.5; Col. 2:13; Mt. 6:14f.; Mk. 11:25), and the enmity and wrath resulting from sin. This sinister breach runs through the entire creation. It is to this that the New Testament message of reconciliation is addressed. Its basic affirmation is that in the life of Jesus God himself stepped into this breach with the purpose of reconciling sinful and therefore ruined creation by making his Son, himself, 'sin' (2 Cor. 5:21). Reconciliation is the goal of Christ's whole life. In every dimension of his life he is the mediator (1 Tim. 2:5; Heb. 8:6; 9:15; 12:24). But it is above all in his suffering and death that the *fact* of his role as mediator and reconciler becomes visible. The *cross of Christ,* Christ's sacrifice, therefore, is of decisive importance in the reconciling event. The cross is the 'efficient cause' of our reconciliation.

5. It is in this light that we are to understand and strive for the transformation of our human world. Since peace between God and humanity is established in the cross of Christ, reconciliation in our human world means our calling, our mission, to establish peace. The task is a quite concrete one: the Christian *community* becomes *a place of reconciliation.* Paul is noticeably fond of speaking of reconciliation in the first person plural. This means that both life within the Church and the Church's mission to the world are set within the horizon of the event of reconciliation. The very visible and even sociologically recognizable consequences of reconciliation are most clearly articulated in the epistle to the Ephesians. In Christ, the dividing 'wall' between

the 'far off' and the 'near' has been broken down. The Church's privilege and obligation, therefore, is to show itself to be the Church by venturing across the sociological, cultural and religious boundaries. The 'ecumenical' initiative is thus built-in to the community of Jesus from the very beginning. The social mission of Christians can only be understood as 'service of reconciliation', as service for peace. Christians who ignore this mission, in their personal relations with other human beings, in marriage and family life, for example, or in their church life, but also in their particular society and political context, are not merely failing to live in accord with the salvation Christ has established as reconciliation but giving it the lie direct.

6. We catch sight here of a special *challenge* of the New Testament idea of reconciliation. While reconciliation is proclaimed and practiced explicitly in the Christian *community,* it cannot be restricted to the circle of Christians but takes place in a framework which is truly cosmological. When Paul asserts in *Colossians:* 'Through him God chose to reconcile *the whole universe* to himself . . . . to reconcile all *things,* whether on earth or in heaven, through him alone' (Col. 1:20), this is not just a poetical flourish. This stress on the universal reach of the work of reconciliation is to be taken seriously. 'Reconciliation must be thought of in the widest possible sense. Just as the created universe was "subjected to *vanity*" for our sakes and now "waits with eager expectation for God's sons to be revealed" (Rom. 8:18ff.), so too, the peace established by God embraces the non-human creation and even the rebellious cosmic powers. In Johannine terms, from the standpoint of an even more radical condemnation of the cosmos: God loved the cosmos so much

and in such a way that he sent his Son so that everyone who has faith in him may not die but have eternal life (Jn. 3:16)' (Weber).[38] We must keep this formulation in mind: deliverance is not something which happens automatically but is inseparable from faith. But this faith always relates reconciliation to the world and never exclusively to itself. The 'ministry of reconciliation' is poles apart from the satisfaction of the private needs of Christians obsessed with their own salvation. This ministry of reconciliation is a charge to promote reconciliation in the world and for the world.

Traditional Theories of Reconciliation

Starting from this New Testament basis, how did the doctrine of reconciliation develop in the Church? This development has a long history and is not easily traced. One striking fact is that, despite the substantial centrality of the message of reconciliation in the Bible, the early Church and its theologians felt no necessity to develop this message into a fully-orbed doctrine. 'Redemption in Jesus Christ was one of the central tenets of faith which never became a matter for *direct* and *explicit* doctrinal definition. Indeed, down to Anselm's day, only in a rudimentary way did it become a theme of theological speculation or *explicit* dispute in the schools. The doctrine of redemption consequently remained at the pre-reflective level of straight biblical proclamation, liturgical celebration and Christian experience, far more and far longer than did other comparable Christian convictions. This made possible the development of a far greater diversity and even disorder' (Greshake).[39]

Certain prominent New Testament motifs were to hand as the 'raw material' for tentative doctrinal forays. Emil Brunner refers in his *Dogmatics* to the

81

following five motifs: 'The *first* element of interpretation was offered by the sacrificial cultus of the Old Testament . . . . and the connected idea of atoning sacrifice' ('The picture of the vicarious suffering of the "servant of the Lord" in Isaiah 53 was the link between Christ's death on the cross and the atoning sacrifice'). At the same time, the Book of Isaiah also offered a *second* possible interpretation of Jesus' death on the cross as a reconciling event: namely, the idea of 'penal suffering: . . . . "The chastisement of our peace was upon him" and "the Lord hath laid on him the iniquity of us all"'. 'There was, however, a *third* view: . . . . that of guilt and the idea of a "bond": "the bond written in ordinances against us" —a figure taken from the sphere of civil law—the "law of contract", we would say today . . . . He is the "Righteous Servant" (who) "goes bail" for us . . . . He redeems us" and indeed "pays" at the cost of His life, and in this act sets us free . . . .'

The *fourth* sphere is 'where the idea of atonement is replaced by that of redemption (inseparable from it)'. 'The cross achieves a real *spolatio hostium,* which ends in the triumphal procession of the victor'. 'God through Christ rescues the booty, by delivering man from "the power of darkness" . . . . into God's keeping'.

Fifthly, Christ's sufferings and death on the cross could be interpreted as 'the true Paschal Sacrifice or Passover'. 'In the blood of Jesus the New Covenant is established, the new Exodus. "The blood of the New Covenant" is not only the sign but also the means by which the new relation with God, the new communion with God is created' (E. Brunner).[40]

All five motifs are essential ingredients in the New Testament message. All of them orbit around the one great central theme: the passion and death of Jesus on the cross. But they do so from different positions and in this way illustrate the complexity of the New Testament centre. All five are important for the Church's thought and witness. At the same time their very diversity is a safeguard against any impatience to impose a fixed pattern on the theme of reconciliation. 'In the way it bears witness to the doctrine of reconciliation especially, therefore, Holy Scripture proves an antidote to any temptation to systematize in an unduly rigid manner' (Greshake).[41]

Gradually, however, faith's quest for understanding began even in the area of the doctrine of reconciliation and redemption, although there were none of the dramatic confrontations which characterized the development of the christological or trinitarian dogmas and no exceptional sense of urgency or obligation. Different approaches and options found expression in different versions of the doctrine of reconciliation but the relatively distinctive and conflicting features of these versions never completely ruled out the others. These versions can be classified in a variety of ways. The classification proposed by the Swedish theologian Gustaf Aulén in the nineteen thirties still seems to me to be one of the most successful. Without ignoring other views, I shall adopt the main lines of Aulén's presentation basing my outline on his major study: *Christus Victor, An historical study of the three main types of the idea of the atonement.*[42]

According to Aulén, the course of Christian doctrine has produced essentially *three* typical theories of atonement, with a wide variety of detailed interpretation within each type.

1) The *classical theory*, as first formulated by the Greek fathers and subsequently radicalized by Luther.

2) The *Latin theory*, as proposed by Cyprian and, above all, by Anselm and widely adopted by Reformation orthodoxy.

83

3) The *subjective, humanist type* of theory of the atonement, as adumbrated by Abelard in the medieval period and becoming dominant in theological modernism since the Enlightenment. We turn to these three types of atonement theory for a closer look.

Aulén's own clear preference is for the first type. He calls it the 'classical' theory because it was the first to emerge as a distinctive theory of the atonement in the writings of the early church fathers, above all in Irenaeus and the great Cappadocian fathers. The basic feature of this classical theory of the atonement is indicated in the title of Aulén's book: *Christus Victor*. The work of reconciliation is the struggle and victory of Christ. The world view underlying this conception tends to see the world as as the scene of a dramatic struggle between two hostile powers. Human history, indeed the whole cosmos, is enslaved by the powers of destruction. In the early Church these powers were identified primarily as sin, death and the devil. By the fall of humanity into sin, they have seized power in the cosmos. As long as they dominate the world, the hostility between God and humanity remains and the human race is imprisoned in a two-fold, indeed three-fold, alienation: enslaved to sin, subjected to the stronger demonic forces, and threatened by God's wrath and judgement. It is a vicious circle. There is no deliverance from this alarming situation through forces immanent in our world. We are no match for these powers which alienate us. No 'exodus' is possible for the sinful cosmos in its own strength. The chief reason for this is that this situation is also a culpable one since the 'principalities and powers' have seized power over us not altogether without justification, not entirely unaided by us. The vicious circle can only be broken from outside, therefore, and indeed from a quite specific 'outside' and by the only real 'Outsider', the only one who is really 'outside' this alienated world, i.e. by God the Creator.

According to the New Testament, this is exactly what happened in Christ. In him God's 'exodus' towards humankind took place, leading God right down into the depths of our servitude, the conditions of which are so graphically described in the synoptic accounts of the way Jesus exorcized the demons and explored so profoundly by Paul in his fundamental reflections on the resurrection and the way this reaches even into the domain of the principalities and powers. For Christ, this journey of the Son of God into the far country entailed a life and death struggle. It cost him his life. He died on the cross. Yet this cross in particular, far from being a tragedy, was the scene of Christ's victory.

The drama of the cross was depicted in constantly changing and sometimes very vivid images in the church fathers (and Luther). The devil is unable to hold the innocent Jesus in his deadly clutches. He loses his 'case'. He is 'outwitted' by Christ because he fails to see the divinity concealed in the manhood. At the very point where the devil seems to have achieved his supreme and final triumph, i.e. at the cross of Christ, he is undone. From then on, his kingdom is a shattered, condemned and conquered kingdom, *de iure,* and *de facto*. As a result, the basic constitution of our world has been transformed; a real 'revolution' takes place. The prisoners of creation are redeemed, liberated, their imprisonment ended; they are released, given a new lease of life. The exodus of the human race, the whole cosmos, from death to life has now become a possibility and a reality. And the final message of this event of salvation: the fatal divisive state of hostility between God and the world comes to an end; God reconciles the world with himself.

Many features of this classical theory of the atonement are overdrawn and sometimes crudely exaggerated, and with the passage of time they have become strange and largely unacceptable to us today. Not surprisingly this theory has had a bad press in the recent history of theology (though this was already true to some extent in the medieval period as well). This was especially the case with Protestant theology. Objection was rightly taken to the crude mythology of this classical theory; the imagery and terminology needed to be 'demythologized'. The theory was criticized as too 'objectivistic', too 'automatic': the reconciling event takes place here almost 'above our heads' in the battle between God and the devil. We human beings seem to be no more than a 'bone of contention', even mere puppets at the mercy of the supernatural powers. There is some substance in this criticism, too, even if certain nuances need to be included in its presentation. It is hardly possible for us to commit ourselves to this classical theory today or even to adopt uncritically Aulén's clear preference for it.

Yet Aulén's plea for greater sympathy towards this classical type of soteriology deserves respect and attention. Not merely as a timely corrective to certain deep-rooted prejudices in our attitude to church history but also in the interests of a systematic approach to soteriology today. This theory of salvation as reconciliation has its strong points which need to be remembered today. Let me mention just three of them:

1. Leaving aside the crude or 'grotesque' (Aulén's own term) terminology employed in this world-view, we must nonetheless take its realistic, universalist,

vision of reality seriously. This vision is *realistic* because its view of alienation in human life is strict and inclusive. The whole world lies in the power of the Evil One (1 Jn. 5:19) and endlessly moves in its 'vicious circles'; yet we are not to take a fatalistic view of this hopeless situation. What underlies this alienation is not some unalterable Fate but human sin — the concrete sins of each one of us. Only this sin is no mere 'incident' to be interpreted moral-istically, explained and trivialized in individualistic terms. On the contrary it is a plunge into enmity against the Creator, separation from him and consequently a betrayal of his creation; in other words, a 'clearance sale' whereby the good gifts of the creation are sold off to and expropriated by the devil as the power of alienation.

Here the *universalist* character of this vision becomes plain. According to the classical theory of atonement, the human being is not just an isolated individual. He or she is inseparably related to cosmic dimensions and this relationship is also reciprocal. Human freedom is limited by these dimensions; the human being is a limited and conditioned being, a 'fellow-creature'. But conversely, the exercise of human freedom and responsibility (and also their misuse) involves our environment in our human suffering. There is a dimension of solidarity, therefore, a cosmic and ecumenical dimension, in this theory of the atonement, inseparable from its realism. In the history of Christian doctrine this emphasis has not always been maintained. Certainly not enough attention has been given to it in modern Protestantism with its moralizing individualistic view of reconciliation. But it is assuming a new impor-tance today.

2.   Especially important in this classical theory of

atonement, to my mind, is its central motif, namely, its emphasis on the *sovereignty of the active and committed love of God*. This work of reconciliation is wholly God's idea. He is the sole subject of this work. He does not wait until certain conditions are met before reconciling the world to himself. There are no strings attached. He attaches no provisos in the shape of things his creatures must do in return for reconciliation. He is the subject of reconciliation and in no sense its object. Even the central concept of sacrifice is to be understood in this sense within the context of reconciliation. Sacrifice is not a cultic transaction: not a *do ut des* (I give that you may give). To restore unity in this sin-corrupted world certainly demands sacrifice. But this sacrifice is 'offered' by God himself. It is he himself who undertakes it. He is *victor quia victima,* the victor because he is the victim.

The term 'objectivist' has frequently been applied to this theory of atonement and its approach. Rightly so, if by 'objectivist' is meant that the reconciliation takes place *extra nos*. Wrongly so, if it means that the work of atonement is to be understood as an almost 'mechanical' impersonal operation 'from above'. But there is no ground for asserting this of the classical theory of atonement. In the thinking of the church fathers, God's sovereignty is no objectivist mechanical process but the sovereignty of his active committed love. God does not allow his creation to perish, does not leave mankind to stew in its own juice. On the contrary, he enters into our situation, acts decisively in struggle and conflict, in suffering and compassion and death. His reconciliation is unconditional because his love is unconditional in its solidarity with us in struggle and in suffering. In the deepest sense, therefore, the *extra nos* of the atonement is a *pro nobis.*

All other considerations and aspects which may arise in the Christian doctrine of reconciliation are, of course, governed by this unconditional *pro nobis*: for example, the legal order violated by sin which requires to be restored in the work of reconciliation. Aulén rightly says: 'The legal order can no longer have the final and supreme word in God's relationship to mankind. This final and supreme word is spoken, on the contrary, by the self-giving self-sacrificing love of God which breaks through the legal order.[43] Breaks through it not in any wilful and arbitrary way but for the sake of his creatures in an act of divine faithfulness towards mankind. Undoubtedly the classical approach to the idea of reconciliation and the orientation it gives to that idea reproduces biblical elements faithfully and dynamically.

3.   The last remark also applies to the third point I want to mention as a special strength of this classical theory of the atonement, namely, the close *connection it makes between reconciliation and liberation*. The 'logic' of its striking drama is as follows: What is at stake in the conflict between God and the demonic powers is the deliverance of humanity from the tyrannical forces of destruction. Yet even when these dramatic ideas are not to the fore, even when careful and even guarded thinkers use theological and metaphysical arguments here (to such an extent that some have permitted themselves to talk mistakenly — here of all places! — of 'naturalistic' tendencies in the view of salvation, even here, on closer inspection, the soteriological thrust appears. To take one example, from Irenaeus: 'The Word of God was made flesh in order that he might destroy death and bring man to life; for we were tied and bound in sin, we were born in sin and live

under the dominion of death'.[44] What is at stake is mankind's eternal and therefore also its temporal life, exodus from the dominion of death and therefore, in the deepest sense, the redemption and liberation of the creation, in the all-inclusive sense affirmed so matchlessly in the eighth chapter of Romans. The classical theory of the atonement deserves to be taken very very seriously today not least for its vision of reconciliation as liberation.

Given the diversity of biblical motifs and also the diverse historical contexts within which the question of salvation is wrestled with, this classical theory of the atonement could not possibly remain alone in the field. Quite early on in the history of the ancient Church, another theory was developed, namely the Latin theory, to which we now turn. The transition from a Greek social context to a Latin one had inevitable consequences. The new cultural environment provided theological questions with a new setting. From the very beginning a new course was set even for the development of the Latin type of atonement theory. In the case of the classical theory, the influence at work in the cultural background was the problem of alienation in a world threatened by principalities and powers, by mortality and death, i.e. primarily the problem of cosmic soteriology. In the case of the Latin theory, the influence which was to the forefront was the question of a legal order in a world of sinful human beings. The two trends are not simple opposites but they do indicate a shift of emphasis.

This shift is already palpable in Tertullian. Being a lawyer, he found it impossible to consider our relationship to God in isolation from the legal question this necessarily raised. 'How absurd it is to leave the penance unperformed and yet expect

90

forgiveness of sins! What is it but to fail to pay the price and nevertheless to stretch out the hand for the benefit! The Lord has ordained that forgiveness is to be granted for this price. He wills that the remission of the penalty is to be purchased for the payment which penance makes'.[45] The theological principle *aut satisfactio aut poena* (either satisfaction or penalty) holds good with no exceptions. This view, formulated in the context of penitential practice, was transformed by Cyprian to the doctrine of reconciliation. Christ's atoning work was interpreted analogously to penitential practice: Christ's sacrifice is a compensatory satisfaction provided by God for sin.

It was Anselm of Canterbury who first developed the idea of atonement as satisfaction into a full-fledged theory. We now turn for a closer look at his theory. Our primary source here is his *Cur Deus homo?* (composed 1094-1098). As the title indicates, Anselm's object in this work is to understand and expound the logic of the divine incarnation, and indeed, to do so in the strictly rational sense of demonstrating the inherent necessity for the incarnation. This was to be done *remoto Christo* (apart from Christ), i.e. by an attempt to interpret the *ratio* of the event of Jesus Christ, not that event itself. (We must be careful not to misunderstand this approach of Anselm in a 'rationalist' sense, as this term is nowadays understood. The style of Anselm's thinking is that of medieval realism. The idea has a 'real' significance attached to it, therefore, not just a 'nominal' one. And what is at stake here is, meta-physically, the supreme and absolutely real Being. This gives Anselm's essay a very special intellectual and existential status and dignity. It is the very essence of faith and intelligence which is at stake here).

How does Anselm develop his argument? The underlying problem of reconciliation is the reality of sin. Anselm's view of the problem of sin is very keen, sharp and impressive. The problem is the *exhonoratio Dei,* the dishonouring of God. It is not just that mankind betrays its Maker by its apostasy and in doing so wrecks the order of creation but that, over and above that, it impugns the *honour of God.* And it is this that shows sin up for what it really is. Far from being merely a trivial incident, merely a superficial and partial disorder, it is actually rebellion against God himself, an assault on his honour. God being God, however, he cannot forfeit his honour and so the consequences of this rebellion rebound upon the creation. 'Human sin impugns what is absolutely unimpugnable. The whole of creation is turned topsy-turvy, therefore . . . . By impugning the unimpugnable honour of the Creator, a wrong is committed which far outweighs all relations within the created world and is quite unique'.[46]

This being so, for Anselm the problem of reconciliation is the problem of the *satisfactio* required, the problem of how this offence against God's honour can be repaired. This is the tip of the iceberg of sin. If reconciliation is to be genuine, it cannot possibly ignore this fact. Tertullian's dictum *aut poena aut satisfactio* is strictly valid. For God the Creator, *punishment* is ruled out, since the punishment of sin is death, and, in view of the cosmic ramifications of the alienation caused by sin, that would mean the destruction of the whole of creation. Because he is the faithful Creator, however, God cannot endorse that solution. The only alternative left him, therefore, is *satisfactio.*

This is not a biblical term but one derived from the penitential practice of the Church (even perhaps from the Germanic judicial system). What are we to make of it? It indicates a public reparation for an offence against someone's honour, an act to be performed by the offending party in order to right the wrong committed against the injured party. In the case of creation, humanity is the guilty party which has impugned the divine honour. Humanity, therefore, must 'pay'. But how and with what? Humanity has nothing with which it could 'pay'. It is the creature which owes everything to God the Creator. Anything it might offer in payment already belongs by right to this Creator, is already owed to him. It would itself be a *debitum* (a debt, an obligation) but certainly not a *meritum* (a merit) which is what *satisfactio* requires if it is to be genuine. The requirements of reconciliation present us with a real dilemma, therefore: only by humanity can reconciliation be accomplished, yet humanity is ruled out in fact as the one subject quite incapable of fulfilling this role.

This is a dilemma which only God can resolve. As in the classical theory of the atonement, he alone is the genuine 'Outsider', outside the vicious circle of sin. He alone, therefore, can break that vicious circle. But, and here the satisfaction theory differs from the classical, only if certain conditions are fulfilled can this breakthrough be expected or understood. God does not circumvent his own order of justice. He cannot simply ignore this impugning of his honour. It is indeed the tip of the iceberg on which the whole of creation is wrecked. There can be no salvation for humanity if this tip of the iceberg is ignored. In some way or other, humanity itself must share in the work of its own reconciliation. But this cannot be done by a human being in the Adamic succession, one descended from the first Adam, but only by the Second Adam, the humanity of God, the 'God-man'. The sole possibility of reconciliation through satisfaction is by God's own presence in humanity, i.e. by his incarnation. Here alone is the answer to the question *Cur Deus homo?* Why the incarnation? Soteriology is the essential motive for christology, the inner ground of and the answer to the question of christology. Conversely, the soteriological answer presupposes the christological question: christology is the presupposition, the basis, of soteriology.

Anselm's theory is an astonishingly coherent and close-knit argument, systematically constructed and developed step by step with great care and stringency. No wonder it had such an influence, especially in the Reformation period and subsequently right down to the present day, as for example in Karl Barth's doctrine of reconciliation. Yet it never lacked its critics, even among Anselm's own contemporaries (as we shall shortly see), right down on into later centuries, particularly in the recent history of Protestant theology. Among the Enlightenment thinkers, especially, Anselm soon joined Augustine and others as the chief bogeymen in the history of Christian doctrine.

This brilliant doctrinal theory does indeed lay itself open to serious criticism. Many aspects both of its form and content strike us as, and indeed are in fact, rebarbative and quite unacceptable. This applies above all, certainly, to the contingent frame of reference of Anselm's theory, largely culturally determined and profoundly medieval in character. Although post-medieval thinkers can understand this aspect, they nevertheless find it strange and alien. This strangeness should not be exaggerated, however, as it has been by many of Anselm's critics in modern Protestantism. To do this, inevitably produces certain caricatures of the theory which are widely current even today. For example, in an otherwise valuable textbook we find the following account of Anselm's view of the atonement: 'God is represented as a king ruling his country. Sin becomes *lèse majesté,* therefore, and an insult to the honour of God . . . . God owes it to himself, so to speak, either to punish this insult to his honour or else demand its expiation . . . . (otherwise) he would lose face as king. God is subject to the pressure of roles, i.e. to the demands of the legal order which must at all costs be upheld'.[47]

This description is unfair to Anselm above all in its use of such emotive phrases as 'lose face' and 'pressure of roles'. The last thing Anselm means by the honour of God is divine egotism or self-regard. It is rather 'that honour which is the foundation of the universal order of justice and peace between God and man and which also means, therefore, man's honour, dignity and peace'.[48] God's concern for his 'honour' is inseparably, at one and the same time, his concern for the fundamental interests of his creation and for its liberation.

We have to be quite clear about this if we are not to indulge in over-simplification. Yet our uneasiness with the framework of Anselm's theory remains. This is not just because we live in a very different cultural milieu from that of the late Middle Ages. It is also because we keep in view the biblical basis of the message of reconciliation. The predominance of legal and logical categories here poses a theological problem. Anselm was unquestionably right to try to translate the biblical message into the context and categories of his time. The Latin culture obviously called for such attempts to develop new theories. But the actual attempt to do so in this framework led to considerable modifications in the biblical view of atonement. We are concerned here, therefore, not just with the formal question of the means of expression and the frame of reference used in Anselm's theory but also with the very material question of how far this theory corresponds with the biblical and theological basis.

Discrimination is called for here too. Not everything which modern theology has often found fault with in Anselm, his 'notorious objectivism', for example, really deserves to be rejected. Anselm's emphasis on the honour of God in the divine action on behalf of a threatened creation is largely in accord with the biblical view of reconciliation. Yet more perhaps than in the classical theory, the presence of distorting elements is evident in the way in which Anselm develops this emphasis. To the question whether Anselmian doctrine of satisfaction really does justice to the sovereignty of God's love in the history of Jesus Christ, I am inclined to answer No. This is not to question Anselm's intention, on his presuppositions and with the means of expression available to him, to witness to the saving initiative of the faithful Creator on behalf of his creation, nor Anselm's actual achievement. There are no grounds whatever for misinterpreting his 'objectivism' in a mechanical sense. The almost inevitable decision of God in favour of the second option when the choice is between *poena* or *satisfactio* is undoubtedly the decision of his eternal love. Yet within the terms of reference of Anselm's doctrine, the sovereignty of this divine love can only be presented in a strangely fragmented fashion.

Comparing Anselm's theory with the classical theory dialectically, Aulén describes this fragmentation as follows: Whereas in the early church fathers, the love of God breaches every legal order by its very superiority, in Anselm the intact legal order in a sense breaches the act of divine love in the work of Christ. 'The whole object of his argument is to show how the Man appears who is able to give the satisfaction which God absolutely demands . . . . The line that leads downwards may be shown as crossed by a line leading from below upwards, to represent the satisfaction made to God by Christ as man. . . . God is . . . *partly* the agent . . . and *partly* the object (sc. of the reconciliation)'.[49] God's love is tied down by conditions, presuppositions, performances. Admittedly, there are good (i.e. appalling) reasons for this, i.e. the destructive power of sin and, in consequence, the appalling distress in which the human race finds itself after the plunge into sin, that sin whose depths Anselm plumbed with a profundity unparalleled in the history of theology. Nor are these conditions of human distress imposed upon God from the outside, so to speak; rather is it his love which imposes them upon himself and chooses therefore to act within their framework. But this is precisely the point: it is only within this framework that it acts and it is the necessity and transparent rationality of this framework which appears to be for Anselm the really interesting and important theological point.

At this point, therefore, we must ask whether this perspective does not seriously distort the concrete event attested in the New Testament account of Jesus Christ. Is it pure chance that behind the rigid structure of Anselm's proof of the inherent necessity of Christ's divine humanity, 'salvation with a human face' is hardly visible at all? Have we not been transported from the realm of evangelical freedom and its dramatic presentation in salvation history into the rarefied atmosphere of a highly sophisticated dogmatic necessity? And even if we accept without qualification that Anselm's impressive system rests on the foundations of evangelical faith and is therefore anything but a speculative alternative to this faith, it seems to me almost beyond doubt that the very structure of this system also obscures much of this evangelical basis. In spite of its great influence in Christian dogmatics, therefore, even this Latin type of atonement theory, which worked out its idea of reconciliation with the strictest possible logic, could not in these circumstances play any dominant role or even deserve to do so.

Theologians continued to work at soteriology, therefore, and produced other theories. Significantly enough, a new soteriological theory appeared even in Anselm's own life time and in the long run proved very influential. It may be described as a third type of theory of the atonement. The raw material for it was assembled by Peter Abelard (1079-1142), the *enfant terrible* of early scholastic theology. In many respects his theory is the counterpoint to Anselm's system. Abelard's theological interests lay in a different direction than Anselm's. What interested him was not so much *satisfactio* in the sense of the bridging of the gulf between God and humanity, the correction of a situation which in God's sight really exists, but rather the consequences of the atonement for the subjective condition of humanity, i.e. the human subject's personal transformation, conversion from sin and emancipation for a life lived in love. It is here, for Abelard that Christ's life and work take on their decisive soteriological significance. All his life but, above all, in his death on the cross, Jesus showed himself to be a compelling witness of love. His authority is demonstrated by his unique capacity to kindle in us love for God and our fellow human beings. The real reconciling work of Christ consists in this *'infectious' power of his love*.

When we come to Abelard with Anselm and the classical theory of the atonement fresh in mind, these are exhilaratingly new accents. The doctrine of the atonement is vigorously switched to another track. The believing Christian with his or her special interest in salvation insists on the right to speak. Nor is this out of place. Abelard brings out certain aspects of the New Testament message far more clearly than did the two previous types of atonement theory. Abelard moves in a world in which we feel far more directly and vividly in contact with the historical Jesus of Nazareth. The Jesus of the synoptic gospels becomes tremendously important. But even references in Paul and the Johannine writings to the constraining love of Christ as the demonstration of God's love also acquire greater significance. For example, Romans 5:8: 'But Christ died for us while we were yet sinners, and that is God's own proof of his love towards us'. Or again, Jn. 15:13: 'There is no greater love than this, that a man should lay down his life for his friends'. It is to Abelard's lasting credit to have put this aspect of the New Testament kerygma right back in the forefront.

The weakness of Abelard's soteriology, however, lay in the somewhat superficial way in which he developed this powerful dimension of the kerygma. This becomes obvious when we compare Abelard's theory with the first two theories. The radical problem which so rightly and so profoundly perplexed those two theories, namely, the problem of the abyss of alienation, the appalling menace to human life from sin and death, this problem appears only on the margins of Abelard's account. But if this radical dimension is treated so superficially in this account, can it possibly reflect faithfully the biblical idea of reconciliation? Can the result be anything other than a trivialization of the biblical vision of salvation in Christ and

99

ultimately even of the love of Christ, the very theme to which Abelard more than any other wished to draw attention? For the New Testament itself does not present this love of Christ exclusively or predominantly as a stimulus to responding love. If we leave out of account the background in the history of salvation, the dimension of eschatological sacrifice and expiation, we can hardly do justice to the love of Christ in all its profundity as attested and embodied in the cross of Christ.

There is a very modern ring in the Abelardian emphases, their graphic qualities and the importance placed upon the subjective aspects of the idea of reconciliation. Nor is it pure chance that this third theory of the atonement should have come into its own only in the modern period. I am thinking especially of its heyday in the neo-Protestant theology of the nineteenth century. Here, too, Schleiermacher was the pacemaker. The 'reconciling work' of the Saviour consisted in his incorporation of believers into 'the fellowship of his perfect blessedness'. Union with Jesus in his blessedness helps us to find peace and happiness in our own inner life. This applies, above all, to the problem of sin. But Schleiermacher sees the problem of sin quite differently from Anselm. It is not so much a question of a dangerous breach and abyss in human life, still less of an affront to the divine honour which we cannot possibly put right, but the problem of our human morosity, of the 'barriers' which disturb and burden sinners in their inner experience, in their failures, in their happiness. Under the influence of Jesus, it is precisely this aspect of sin, this 'morosity' in personal life, these 'barriers' to personal fulfillment, which are radically undermined, so that 'the longer and the more consistently we are motivated by Christ, the more we forget sin'.[50]

'Guilt is something which is best forgotten . . . . It is not guilt which needs to be eradicated but the sense of guilt. It is not man's separation from God which needs to be eradicated, but merely the mistaken opinion that he is separated from God. Reconciliation (or atonement) consists in the clearing up of this misunderstanding, namely that man is not from the very outset already united with God. Certainly it is a long way from Abelard to this modern idealistic argument, but the way is continuous, the idea itself is implicit in the view of Abelard'.[51] The event of reconciliation not merely related — legitimately — to the inner life of the human subject, it is transferred almost completely there, though in Abelard not exclusively. But this means that a legitimate aspect becomes a one-sided emphasis which seriously reduces the biblical idea of reconciliation and even ends up in a one-dimensional view of salvation.

Abiding Relevance of These Theories

We turn now to the implications of all this for our reflection on 'Salvation as Reconciliation'. I want to stress two aspects of this background of the history of Christian doctrine: its dialectical unity and its relevance for our thinking today.

The first aspect, the *dialectical unity* of this triad of theories of reconciliation, hardly requires further explanation since it emerged very clearly in the course of our survey. The three great theories of the atonement — the classical, the Latin and the humanistic — are not mutually exclusive but complementary to one another. But this is far from being a commonplace axiom in the field of Christian dogmatics. There have been (and still are) times and occasions in theology when a clear choice has to be made, decisions taken and separate ways taken.

As examples, I mention christology in the history of the ancient Church, and the doctrine of justification by faith at the time of the Reformation. I pointed out earlier that, in the case of the doctrine of reconciliation, the situation was different. The Church felt no obligation to draw hard and fast lines of dogmatic definition in respect of these three types of atonement theory. The outline I have given shows that the Church was quite justified in taking this line. Out of the wealth of the biblical presentation of reconciliation, the three theories select themes which cannot be brought under the same biblical denominator. Within their particular historical context, they develop these themes in a particular direction, adopting a more or less distinctive position; yet each remains open to discussion. Themes insufficiently taken into account in each case, and the changed cultural context of each new age call for a fresh approach and readjustments. Thus, in view both of its biblical basis and of the contemporary character of theology, the history of the doctrine of reconciliation remains and should continue to be seen as a relatively *open enterprise*.

Down to the present day, the three types of atonement theory continue to be *relevant* to us *as guidance*. It was not accidental that these three theories were developed. The solutions they offer are all historically conditioned, of course. In the case of the Latin theory, for example, the presence of particular cultural and social interests and contemporary patterns of thought is palpable. Yet the choice is never completely arbitrary. All three theories latch on to basic themes of the biblical witness to reconciliation. Though different from each other, these themes are nonetheless mutually consistent. It is precisely this characteristic which gives these three theories their importance as guides.

By their very distinctiveness, they bar the way to any attempt to develop a 'reduced' one-sided soteriology. They are a standing invitation to us to 'keep talking to each other', to keep our ears open for essential themes even when vested theological or cultural interests keep them away from the spotlight. To illustrate this point, let me select one emphasis from each of the three types of theory which seems to be particularly relevant for our enquiry.

1. I would strongly emphasize the abiding relevance of the *Christus Victor* theme of the classical theory, for this is the nerve of the Christian message of redemption: its witness to the sovereign love of God which refuses to abandon the world of sin and death in all its alienated darkness but, on the contrary becomes involved in it even to its direst consequences, suffers for it, strives for it, and in conquering it liberates it. These are the strong, disturbing but liberating keynotes of the biblical Gospel. A Christian doctrine of reconciliation cannot ignore them. Neither, therefore, can it ignore the confession of faith 'Christus Victor!', or, in Blumhardt's version, 'Jesus is Victor!' — not just as a verbal statement of belief, of course, but with all the consequences this confession carries with it: namely, commitment to the reconciliation and liberation of the world, a world which on the basis of this confession cannot be abandoned fatalistically to destruction and death.

2. The theologian will do well to pay heed to Anselm's concern. I say the 'theologian' advisedly, for much is to be learned here about the theologian's special business: unswerving fidelity to the task not only of confessing the Gospel of reconciliation but also that of studying it believingly in the

contemporary historical context and making use of the instruments available in that context. With Anselm's example before us, we must at once add that it is not just a question of training in *professio* but also, retroactively, of training in *confessio,* too. To seek the 'logic' (the 'theo-logic') of the Christ-event is not only beneficial to the intellect but also to faith itself. To seek this 'logic' not in order to 'fathom it' or 'get to the bottom of it', nor to 'substantiate' it: *this* theme exists in its own right, its own strength, independently. But in its very sovereignty it is no 'blind' *factum brutum;* as an event, it is an invitation to intelligent faith to seek the underlying presuppositions and consequences of this event. That was what Anselm tried to do and in doing so set us an example, not only for the form of our quest but even for its substance. I am thinking here, for example, of the uncompromising seriousness with which he faced up to the consequences of human sin. With his insistence that 'you have not yet measured the full weight of sin' (*nondum considerasti quanti ponderis sit peccatum*) he established formal and material standards for any Christian doctrine of reconciliation.

3. In view of the contemporary foci of theological attention, it is easier for most of us today to see the relative relevance of the third type of atonement theory, the humanistic Abelardian theory. Let me mention, however, the concern which seems to me the most important here: concern for the impact of the atonement *in our world*. To understand the biblical event of reconciliation as a transaction — a 'happening' — between heaven and earth would be to misunderstand it. Certainly it is a drama which takes place 'between heaven and earth', i.e. between God and humanity, but it is anything but a

'happening' hovering above our heads in some no-man's-land between heaven and earth! Established in Jesus Christ, the atonement is an 'earthly drama'; it deals with us human beings as we are, transforms our situation, makes *metanoia* and renewal possible for us. Understood as the Bible requires us to understand it, the concern of the doctrine of reconciliation is not just to 'interpret' the world (that too, of course!) but also to 'change' it.[52] Champions of the 'humanistic' theory of the atonement have understood better than most others the practical implications of the atonement for our human life here and now. To be sure, they have often taken a narrow and restricted view of these implications, focussing primarily and often almost exclusively on the conditions and motions of our *inner* human world. It is here that the question must be pressed further today. The atonement has implications not just for our inner human world but also for our outer, public, world too. The Christian vision of reconciliation has practical ethical and even political consequences. To see and to champion these consequences is an essential inseparable aspect of 'salvation as reconciliation'.

Ethical and Political Priority of Reconciliation

That brings me to the problem to which I want to devote the remainder of this chapter: *the ethical dimension of the doctrine of reconciliation*. This question receives scant attention in most doctrinal essays. This is true of all three types of atonement theory as well as of the relevant chapters in recent textbooks on dogmatics. It can partly be explained, of course, by saying that dogmatics is not ethics. But this explanation is not altogether satisfactory. The ethical dimension is certainly there in the biblical approach to reconciliation. I refer the reader to my earlier analysis of the New Testament concept of reconciliation. The atonement achieved within our human world is the basis for the commission to work for reconciliation and peace.

1. *Reconciliation as a Priority*

At a key point in the Sermon on the Mount, the following vivid saying of Jesus is recorded: 'If, when you are bringing your gift to the altar, you suddenly remember that your brother has a grievance against you, leave your gift where it is before the altar. First go and make your peace with your brother, and only then come back and offer your gift' (Mt. 5:23f. NEB). Reconciliation with our fellow human beings is here made the *conditio sine qua non* of true worship. Even at the most solemn of moments the necessity for reconciliation calls us away from the altar. What Jesus says here applies to all our 'religious' life. The saying of Jesus is placed in the Sermon on the Mount at the very point where the radical demands of Jesus in respect of the commandment, 'Do not commit murder' are formulated. There are two stages in Matthew's interpretation of this commandment. In the first, Jesus stresses that God's commandment is breached not only by murder but also by anger with a brother, and 'cursing' a brother. In the second stage, verses 23 and following, particularly important in our present context, Jesus says that to fulfil the sixth commandment it is not even enough to avoid anger and cursing. The radical will of God is satisfied only by 'reconciliation'. The 'murderer', therefore, is not just one who commits murder nor even one who is angry, but also the one who neglects and despises opportunities of reconciliation and who, by that very failure, is already under suspicion of murder and accused of murder. This is what I mean when I

106

speak of the priority of reconciliation. 'Nothing takes precedence over reconciliation with your brother . . . . Reconciliation is the opposite pole of murder; it is as creative as murder is destructive'.[53] In other words, the Christian ethic is an ethic of reconciliation. 'Only what is said, done and suffered in the service of reconciliation to the world can therefore be described as "Christian"' (Moltmann).[54] The readiness for reconciliation and the service of reconciliation are what determine whether a life, a movement, a programme, a party are 'Christian' or not.

2. This priority of reconciliation is not to be mistaken for an *ideology of reconciliation*. The Christian concept of reconciliation is not a general idea which can be extended at will. It is rooted in the Christ event. From this event, above all from the cross, it derives its distinctive binding features. It cannot be identified, therefore, with a desire for appeasement, with facile and vain promises, with a spurious peace which avoids conflicts, conceals real tensions, glosses over real injustices.

To avoid the specious errors of a false ideology of reconciliation, we need to remember the doctrinal theories of atonement. The first two types of theory provide a particularly firm basis of criticism. The classical theory mercilessly exposes the dramatic conflicts raging in the alienated creation. The Latin theory leaves no refuge from the question of justice in a legal and world order ravaged by sin. Both theories bear witness to a 'costly reconciliation' — to the appalling price paid by God for salvation in the cross of Christ. There is no sentimentality in the Christian view of reconciliation, therefore; no enthusiasm based on superficial arguments and unctuously moralizing pious wishes and illusions. A ministry of reconciliation which is instructed by the Bible is alert to the demonic strategies of the principalities and powers, considers them critically, and soberly remembers the hidden motives, refusing to evade them or to disguise them. But also, and above all, a Christian ministry of reconciliation refuses to capitulate to these powers, refuses to abandon the field to them. Although the Christus Victor approach provides no optimistic explanation of the world, it does open up the perspective of the eschatological hope, in which these powers have already been demythologized, stripped of their fateful character, and forfeited all right to be regarded as ultimately decisive factors and can and should, therefore, be constantly challenged and called in question. This is the horizon within which conflicts must be faced and endured — with courage and, of course, with our eyes on the reconciliation established and revealed in Christ and coming to us in him. A genuine Christian ministry of reconciliation will be characterized by a hopeful and inventive realism.

3.   While the ministry of reconciliation is personal in its approach, it is also concerned with *conditions and systems*. I pointed out earlier how, in the New Testament view of reconciliation, the reconciliation event as the Christ event is attested and to be understood personally. God's own approach to us in the incarnation is personal. And in the life, death and resurrection of Jesus, he appeals to the individual person and seeks an individual personal response. But the individual is a member of the community. The question of personal salvation is concerned with relationships in family, community and society.

An outstanding feature of the exhortatory

passages in the apostolic letters of the New Testament is the way they insist forcefully on illustrating the implications of the reconciliation established and bestowed in Christ in personal relationships and in the life of the Church. Quarrels, apparently even quite minor ones, between particular individuals and groups are regarded as important enough to be dealt with; they are not religiously unimportant trivialities in comparison with the eschatological importance of Christ's atoning work. Quite the contrary! The light of reconciliation shines in on the human — only too human — life of the congregations and is meant to operate there with transforming, renewing and, in fact, reconciling power. For example, we find the great *carmen Christi* (Phil. 2:5-11) applied to the tensions within the Christian community at Philippi, and there is a similar example in the case of the community in Corinth.

But the matter does not rest there, with an individual approach confined to personal relationships. The reconciling event also has liberating consequences for the structure of the Christian community, for its 'church order'. In the long run the Church of Christ can never be content to establish itself as a permanently structured and self-enclosed entity based on the divisions of race, nationality, culture and sex. It is the Body of Christ, an organic unity composed of many members. In the Church of Christ, therefore, all 'walls of separation' (Eph. 2:14) are to be challenged and broken down as a matter of principle. The magnificent reflections on this theme in the second chapter of the letter to the Ephesians constitute the *magna carta* of every legitimate church order; they also enlarge our view to include structural aspects of the Church's common life. We are to strive for an *ecumenical order of reconciliation* — a task which has not always or everywhere been faithfully carried out in the Church. How often the Church has been structured as a racial church, a class church, a cultural church and a national church, and in addition gone on to seal itself off from others behind these illegitimate walls. Yet the fundamental and inalienable dynamic of the Gospel of reconciliation constrains Christians again and again, despite all their inertia, to join in the liberating movement leading to awareness of the reconciling unity and to its practical achievement.

This inevitably has consequences for the Church's service *for the world*. We recall again that God's reconciliation is meant for the world. The response of the Church to that reconciliation, therefore, its own 'ministry of reconciliation' cannot be confined to the inner life of the Church. This brings the cosmopolitan and *political arena* within the scope of the ministry of reconciliation. Far from being foreign to the message and theology of reconciliation, this arena is present from the very beginning, in precisely those 'mythological' images of the classical theory of the atonement: with the tremendous realism of these ancient images, the sovereign love of Christ is related to the unfathomable dimensions of our human life and, indeed, of the very cosmos itself. The Gospel of reconciliation is not separated from the world of the principalities and powers but actually related to it.

For us today, this means that even at the level of power politics and the, to some extent, really apocalyptic threats to the human race and the whole creation, Christians must do their thinking in the light of the atonement. Not that this light provides us with any ready-made nostrums for a policy for peace, development and the environment. The fact that Christians are entrusted with the Gospel of reconciliation does not mean that they are transformed into official 'insiders' with special access to knowledge. Christians should be the first to recognize this. A certain hesitancy in producing and offering 'advice' is advisable. The message of reconciliation can and must, however, be transposed into political terms; not in the form of 'law' or 'utopianism', of course, but certainly as a binding Gospel, as an initiative for peace and reconciliation, as an encouragement to 'concrete utopias', to the analysis, exposure and dismantling of ways of thinking and social structures which reflect wilful intransigence and injustice, to the patient search for possibilities of establishing genuine reconciliation and peace, to the extension and development of such possibilities at every political level.

Although this way is a long and difficult one, it is far from being an absurd venture, as the history of the Church in spite of everything has again and again demonstrated in earlier as well as in more recent times. The truth is that when Christians have been resolute and faithful in their task of reconciliation, this has often proved to be a genuine and lasting contribution even in the political field. I have in mind here ecumenical efforts for peace, the contribution of the 'historic peace churches' (Mennonites, Quakers, Brethren Church), the movement associated with Martin Luther King, the initiatives taken by the Fellowship of Reconciliation and other groups, the campaign conducted by the women of Northern Ireland, the efforts of German church groups for reconciliation with Eastern Europe, and many others. To dare to suggest the priority of reconciliation even amid the heat and fury of everyday political life has always been the best 'Christian' policy as well, even when the established 'Christian' parties have not always been in accord. I am thinking here of the example of a man like Gustav Heinemann.[55]

Realistic but energetic commitment in this field is undoubtedly an indispensable dimension of 'salvation as reconciliation', part and parcel of our response to its basic affirmation that 'God was in Christ reconciling the world to himself, . . . and he has entrusted us with the message of reconciliation' (2 Cor. 5:19).

4

Salvation as Liberation

The World's Agenda

One of the most striking features of recent ecumenical theology is the strong *emphasis on liberation* as an essential dimension of salvation. This emphasis is something relatively new in the history of doctrine, especially in the history of soteriology. Only relatively new, since if we keep the biblical basis of salvation in view it is impossible to ignore completely the theme of freedom which echoes in the Christian view of salvation. This is especially evident in the biblical concept of *'redemption'*. The root meaning of this term 'to redeem' brings it very close to such verbs as 'release', 'rescue', 'liberate'. The reference here is to quite concrete forces and conditions which threaten to enslave human beings: disease and death, slavery and oppression, calumny and persecution. In this sense redemption becomes almost a synonym for liberation, as may be inferred in particular from the Old Testament terms *'padä'* and *'ga'al'* (but also in the New Testament *'apolutrosis'*). 'Redemption in the Old Testament is an act of Yahweh performed by him in deep solidarity with his people . . . . as an act of "ransoming" or "purchasing" of freedom. Yahweh summons all his incomparable strength to deliver his people from its state of servitude and to set it free'.[56]

Not surprisingly this concrete biblical approach and this indissoluble connection between redemption and liberation was reflected in the history of doctrine; but very soon and surprisingly often it came to be spiritualized. The keyword 'liberation' in consequence lost its concrete historical reference and other 'more spiritual' terms pushed it into the background in doctrinal theories.

Salvation as 'liberation' is enjoying a real comeback today. How is this new development in the history of theology to be explained? One obvious place to look for an answer to this question is the *contemporary cultural background*. We live in a time when the longing for liberation has become vitally important for large sections of humanity—in all 'three worlds'. We have only to remember the year 1968, without question the most dramatic year of the last decade. In all three worlds—in France, Czechoslovakia, the USA and many developing countries—that year was dominated by an urgent cry for freedom and development in the social and cultural fields. Even the *churches,* the ecumenical movement in particular, were seized by the longing for renewal. It was also in 1968 that the Uppsala Assembly of the World Council of Churches took place and the fact that the theme chosen for this Assembly was the text: 'Behold, I make all things new!' was certainly no accident. Nor was it mere chance that, in the field of *theology,* this same year saw the publication of works such as Käsemann's *Jesus Means Freedom,* Moltmann's 'Revolution of Freedom', Ebeling's 'Liberated by Faith', Gutierrez's *A Theology of Liberation* and Cone's *Black Theology of Liberation.*

114

The popularity of the theme of liberation in contemporary soteriology must also be understood against the background of contemporary bids for freedom which though already meeting with tough resistance are hardly yet defeated. The leading theologians of the liberation school of theology have been quite aware of this influence. Gustavo Gutierrez, for example, entitles an early section of his book: 'Theology as a Critical Reflection on Praxis', in which he deals with methodology. He writes: 'A broad and deep aspiration for liberation inflames the history of mankind in our day, liberation from all that limits or keeps man from self-fulfilment; liberation from all impediments to the exercise of freedom'.[57] Although Gutierrez's primary concern is with pre-revolutionary conditions in the Third World, he points incidentally to the situation in the industrialized countries in order to show that this longing for freedom is universal. In these industrialized countries, of course, a genuine pre-revolutionary situation does not exist, the conditions there being in fact 'developed'; but the question of freedom is nevertheless being raised even there, especially among sensitive young people of both sexes. Gutierrez writes: 'Proof of this awareness of new and subtle forms of oppression in the heart of advanced societies! . . . . In them subversion does not appear as protest against poverty but rather against wealth'.[58]

Such a close correspondence with social and cultural trends prompts the question whether, by emphasizing the liberation aspect of salvation so strongly, contemporary theology is not guilty of a questionable *accommodation* to current fashions. Is this contemporary 'boom' in the liberation theme a sign that Christian theology is falling over itself in its eagerness to acquire 'relevance' by following current fashion at the expense of its identity and integrity? Is this yet another example of the Christian truth being disposed of at bargain prices in a clearance sale dictated by the arrival of the new season's models? We must treat such questions quite seriously. The history of Christian doctrine is littered with examples of how easily theology and the Church can accept alien and ersatz themes when following the 'spirit of the age' and consequently lose their own authenticity. It is difficult to fault Walter Kasper's comment on this sobering fact: 'Tradition has constantly made this mistake and today there is a danger of making it in a different way; it could be by imperceptibly assimilating the Christian view of freedom to an abstract-liberalistic attitude or—on the other hand—by drawing up a "theology of liberation" and at the same time—as occasionally happens—more or less imperceptibly making a Marxist-inspired situation-analysis the basis of theological statements'.[59]

Wisdom also dictates, of course, that we should examine such critical warnings themselves with very great care. We have to differentiate between different ways of linking up with current concerns, different ways of adopting these concerns, different ways of being 'up to date'. Between the Uppsala and Nairobi Assemblies of the World Council of Churches, there was a lively debate on the slogan *The world provides our agenda*. This slogan had its enthusiastic advocates and its equally fervent critics, each group with its own interpretation of what the slogan meant. Careful discrimination seems to me to be absolutely vital in such cases. If we mean by this slogan that theology and the Church must be prepared to accept themes and criteria dictated by views prevalent in the 'market' at any given time, then the countenancing of such directives whether from 'right' or 'left' — with flirtatious side glances either at the conservative market or the progressive one — would encourage an illegitimate 'affiliation' and shortlived 'alliance', a deliberate or unconscious 'sell out' of the very substance of the faith.

But another way is also open to us, one which shows genuine theological respect for 'the world's agenda': theologians and Christians will examine the actual social and cultural situation at a given moment and develop theology and its themes not in isolation from that situation but in dialogue with their contemporaries. The readiness to do this is one of the legitimate requirements of our theological existence today, indeed, an essential dimension of that existence. A relevant theology — one which is related to and measured by the Gospel — is practiced within a particular temporal horizon. For the Gospel, because it is witness to the Incarnate Word, made flesh in the concrete historical person and life of Jesus of Nazareth, is itself a concrete historical truth with contemporary relevance.

A small booklet by G. Jacob entitled 'The Christian in a Socialist Society' offers a number of reflections on 'theology's frame of reference' which throw light on the question of methodology. Jacob quotes from an official study carried out by theologians in the German Democratic Republic. These theologians are, of course, very much concerned with the problem of legitimate linkage with the concrete circumstances in which they live and with the ideological interpretation which is inseparable from this society. In an attempt to clarify this notion of 'frame of reference' they assert: 'By this term we mean the sum-total of the historical and social factors which find expression in human thought and action in a given historical situation . . .

Because the Word of God does not merely hold forth about God but identifies himself with us in the solidarity of love, the "frames of reference" are always themselves part of the "proclamation" and to respect them is not just a matter of skilful rhetoric but of evangelical realism and Christian obedience'.[60]

In this second sense, too, 'salvation as liberation' is a legitimate theme of soteriology today. Since this theme takes up contemporary concerns and interests, it presents itself to us in the form of the question of the relevance of theological motifs and standpoints today. But it must also take the form of the question as to the authenticity and identity of the Christian witness to salvation. In order to avoid the first and illegitimate kind of linkage ('accommo-dation' and 'up-to-date-ness'), it requires a biblical and theological basis and direction. ' . . . . the meaning of Christian redemption as liberation can be clarified only by asking about the nature of Christian freedom'.[61]

In distinguishing in this context between *'relevance'* and *'identity'* yet at the same time connecting them together, I am making use of theological themes which have been developed by *Jürgen Moltmann* in the first chapter of his book *The Crucified God*. There he says: 'Theologians, churches and Christians are confronted in their Christian life today more than ever with a double crisis: the *crisis of relevance* and the *crisis of identity*. These two crises are complementary. The more theology and the church attempt to become relevant to the problems of the present day, the more deeply they are drawn into the crisis of their own Christian identity. The more they attempt to assert their identity in traditional dogmas, rites and moral notions, the more irrelevant and unbelievable they become'.[62]

But theologians are not to regard this contemporary predicament of theology as an inescapable dilemma which they can only solve by jumping boldly in one direction or the other; i.e. opting either for social, political or psychotherapeutic activism, on the one hand, or for a historic or fundamentalist isolationism, on the other. For, as our survey of the biblical view of salvation has repeatedly shown us, these are not mutually exclusive alternatives. *Tertium datur*. Moltmann himself shows us how the 'dilemma' can be resolved: he points out the still unexploited resources of the biblical and reformation theology of the cross. 'Reflection on the cross' may be expected to lead 'to the clarification of what can be called Christian identity and what can be called Christian relevance, in critical solidarity with our contemporaries'.[63]

In a similar way I would look for the possible significance of a 'theology of liberation', assuming once again, of course, that the theological content of this term is not to be determined by skimming off the best in contemporary liberation processes and ideologies, but only by taking our bearings from the Bible, stimulated by these contemporary movements. This leads on to the following reflections on the biblical view of freedom.

Freedom as a Basic Theme of Biblical Theology

The Old Testament scholar Hans Joachim Kraus writes in his valuable outline of systematic theology, 'Kingdom of God: Kingdom of Freedom': 'The main theme of biblical and Christian faith is the freedom which is not to be clouded or distorted by servile fundamentalist or ecclesiastical ways of thinking, speaking and behaving'.[64]

This dictum must be taken very seriously. It confirms that the theme of freedom is not simply an 'up-to-date' one but also a central biblical one. Reflection on this theme in the context of soteriology is fitting, therefore, in the interests not only of the 'relevance' but also of the 'identity' of the Christian faith.

In this section my concern is with 'freedom as a *basic theme* of biblical theology' not with the 'biblical *concept* of freedom'. The distinction is important. The biblical message of freedom starts not from a concept of freedom but with liberation as an *event, freedom as a gift.* The *concept* of freedom with which we are familiar is clearly derived from the Greeks: *eleutheria, eleutheros*—the free citizen as distinct from the slave in ancient society, above all, in classical Greek society; the inwardly-free, wise man of Stoic philosophy who is master of himself, unlike the inwardly captive individual who is the slave of his passions. Only at a relatively late stage does this concept appear in the Bible; specifically, only when the first contacts were established with the Hellenistic environment. It does not appear at all in the Old Testament. Apart from a single synoptic passage, it is in the writings of Paul that it plays its main role in the New Testament. Taking the Bible as a whole, therefore, the *concept* of freedom makes its historical and literary appearance only on the margins of Scripture. The *reality* of freedom, however, its achievement, freedom as an event, this is attested from the very beginnings and indeed as the very centre of the biblical message. It could even be said that, in the biblical history of salvation, liberation as event is the beginning and the ending.

From this observation certain methodological conclusions follow for a theologically appropriate approach to the theme of liberation. In particular, to approach it merely as a question of the history of a concept is quite inadequate. This explains my dissatisfaction with the article on 'freedom' in Kittel's *Theological Dictionary of the New Testament*.[65] The limitations of the approach *via* the history of concepts are plainly visible here. H. J. Kraus explains why in the following words: 'The New Testament understanding of the concept is related here exclusively to the Hellenic-Hellenistic world. There is no mention at all of the acts of liberation attested in the Old Testament. Terminological theology is blind to events. It constructs a conceptual God, a God to be understood intellectually, and by doing so it rules out any possibility of a faithful interpretation of the New Testament'.[66]

But the Old Testament background becomes more important than ever when we come to reflect on the theme of freedom; not just as a verbal background but as a background of history, deeds, events. It is in these terms that the Bible elucidates the grand theme of freedom. Let me be more explicit.

The theological centre of the Old Testament is a decisive event of liberation: *the Exodus*. The story of that event is recalled in the oldest credal statement of Israel: 'My father was a homeless Aramaean who went down to Egypt with a small company and lived there until they became a great, powerful and numerous nation. But the Egyptians ill-treated us, humiliated us and imposed cruel slavery upon us. Then we cried to the Lord the God of our fathers for help, and he listened to us and saw our humiliation, our hardship and distress; and so the Lord brought us out of Egypt with a strong hand and outstretched arm, with terrifying deeds, and with signs and portents. He brought us to this place and gave us this land, a land flowing with milk and honey' (Deut. 26:5-9).

This Exodus event has continued to be celebrated over and over again in Israel's creed and worship. This was the basis on which the Old Testament faith lived. For Israel, this was the scene of the decisive revelation. It is no accident that the divine name was revealed in the context of the events of the Exodus. In other words, revelation, salvation and redemption are events taking place not in some mythical pre-history, in some metaphysical beyond, or on the mountain tops of mystical ecstasy, but right in the midst of human history and, indeed, in the form of an act of deliverance and liberation within that history, in the Exodus of an oppressed and marginalized people from bondage into freedom, in a 'revolution of freedom'. Israel's Exodus faith and confession certainly point to more than a freedom movement within history and society. What is involved here is an *eschatological revolution* in exactly the same way as later in the New Testament. But this all-embracing eschatological liberation also includes the concern for freedom in history and society. The theme of freedom can certainly never ever be divorced from this religion, this faith.

This is evident from the Old Testament view of God, people and world. Yahweh is the *free God*. He is not bound to any cultus or any sanctuary. It is in this sense that the prohibition of images is to be understood. He is also the liberating God: not an authoritarian tyrant, nor a supernatural government, but, as the introduction to the Decalogue, the summary of Old Testament ethics, strongly emphasizes, 'The Lord your God who brought you out of Egypt, out of the land of slavery'. He is not the 'wholly Other', the 'completely different One' but the 'One who makes all the difference', the 'One who changes everything'.[67] When someone calls upon him in faith and confesses his name, this is not an appeal to sacred magical cosmic structures nor a reminder of the duty of mortals to adapt themselves piously to these structures but rather an appeal to the Exodus event and a reminder of our human right to venture the way to freedom.

The people of this free and liberating God not unnaturally sees itself also as *a community of free people*. Free in a spiritual and religious sense: this is 'God's pilgrim people', an Abrahamitic community which is never embedded fatefully and slavishly once and for all in any culture but transcends them all eschatologically and is able to survive and outlast them through all the crises of its history (and how many crises Israel has survived!). But the freedom of God's people is not to be understood only in a 'religious' sense. This freedom also has social consequences. Among its peers, Israel was the only nation in which the existence of slavery was radically questioned. To be sure, this radicalism was not always matched by performance; the pressure of circumstances very soon led to certain compromises even here. Yet the clear purpose of God for his people continued to remain visible in the unwearying protests of the prophets, in the institution of the Jubilee Year requiring the release of all slaves and, above all in the eschatological promise of final liberation, peace and justice. This people was called to freedom and, indeed, to freedom for all.

The *world,* too, comes to be understood in the light of the Exodus: it is to be interpreted as creation and as history: as creation, since the world is no eternal divine universe. It has been created; its reality is positive, therefore, but only as created reality, i.e. as relative, conditioned, worldly reality. It is also history: not a hurdy-gurdy of physical and metaphysical forces simply repeating the same thing over and over again in an eternal merry-go-round, but an unfinished journey into the future. In a word, in the light of the Exodus, the world is our human world, a world which is open behind and before, both on God's side and on our side. *Mundus liberatus et semper liberandus* (a liberated world always needing to be liberated afresh).

To my mind, this Exodus standpoint of the Old Testament represents *something radically new* in the history of freedom. Israel's near and distant neighbours never thought in this way. In the world of the ancient East and even that of classical antiquity, a very different kind of thinking prevailed, in profoundly different forms. Adopting A. Th. van Leeuwen's term, we might label this type of thinking 'ontocracy':[68] the world is understood as a closed system, as an unalterable chain of being. It has a strictly hierarchical structure and is mythically (or metaphysically) pre-determined. The eternal order predetermines the cosmos and, *via* the cosmos, our human world, too, which is inexorably ruled by the macrocosm. Neither in nature nor society, therefore, is there any real human freedom; we are bonded into, incorporated into the universe.

It was G. W. F. Hegel, it will be recalled, who said of the ancient East (in contrast to Hellenism and Germanic Christianity) that it knew of only one free person, namely, the ruler, and that even he was free only in a qualified sense since in the last analysis even he was the plaything of cosmic forces and free, therefore, only in relation to what was 'below' him but not in relation to the cosmos. Human freedom was almost completely stifled in this ontocratic world, therefore. A new freedom became possible only when this ontocratic stranglehold was broken, only when the cosmos was confronted with God as free Creator, as the 'One who changes everything', only when the people of this God saw itself and behaved as a liberated 'pilgrim people' with its sights set on the future and when the world came to be understood as an 'open-ended' history and fashioned tentatively and experimentally in the light of this future. Precisely this was what happened in the Exodus event and the Exodus faith at the heart of the Old Testament; Israel's faith, therefore, was an authentic *revolution of freedom*.

Exodus: The Radical Heritage of the Old Testament

In seeking to establish the Old Testament basis for 'salvation as liberation', I have relied chiefly on *the Exodus event*. In doing so I am taking a line which is forcefully adopted in current theologies of liberation, where the Exodus theme understandably becomes the real basis for the theological direction they take. Both from the standpoint of systematic theology and that of Old Testament scholarship this use of the Exodus theme faces critical questions or at least correctives. In these theologies of liberation is there not a tendency to exaggerate the importance of the liberation event, to apply it to the field of contemporary social ethics in an unbalanced and sometimes even sectarian way? The Exodus event is surely presented in the Old Testament tradition as only one event among many, and indeed as one which is extraordinarily opalescent in character. Furthermore, has not this esteem for the Exodus event been introduced into contemporary theology from the outside?

Some clarification is called for here and I begin with the last of these questions:

1. It is certainly the case that this great *'discovery'* of the Exodus theme in contemporary theology owed

less to Old Testament scholarship than to the—sometimes very unconventional and astonishing—views of non-theologians, and not least to an atheist intellectual, the Marxist philosopher Ernst Bloch. The word 'discovery' certainly needs to be put in quotes, for the Exodus theme as such was never altogether forgotten in Old Testament theology and ethics. Yet throughout almost the entire history of Christian doctrine, the importance of this theme for soteriology was in fact largely underestimated. The 'enthusiasts' or 'fanatics' of the left-wing of the Reformation (the so-called 'radical reformation'), with their concern to change the world, were the exception to this general rule. Yet these 'radical reformers' never enjoyed much real success, least of all within the German culture. The neglect of the Exodus in Christian doctrine was part of a wider neglect of the Old Testament in general in this area (but not only in this area). H. J. Kraus rightly says of the mainstream of doctrinal history: 'In face of this event (i.e. the Exodus), Christian theology and the Christian Church suffered a fatal and disastrous spiritualization. The Exodus was interpreted as a prefiguration of salvation and in the process lost its relevance for earthly politics'.[69]

In his letters and papers from prison, Dietrich Bonhoeffer pointed out with deep insight the consequences this had for the Christian concept of salvation. Salvation came to be understood in terms of an abstract 'religion of redemption' focussed on private spirituality and the other world. Bonhoeffer comments: 'Unlike the other oriental religions, the faith of the Old Testament isn't a religion of redemption. . . . But isn't this a cardinal error, which separates Christ from the Old Testament and interprets him on the lines of the myths about redemption? To the objection that a crucial importance is given in the Old Testament to redemption (from Egypt, and later from Babylon —cf. Deutero-Isaiah) it may be answered that the redemptions referred to here are *historical,* i.e. on *this* side of death, whereas everywhere else the myths about redemption are concerned to overcome the barrier of death. Israel is delivered out of Egypt so that it may live before God as God's people on earth.'[70]

It is clear from these comments of Bonhoeffer that during the war years Protestant theology was already taking the significance of the saving events of the Exodus more seriously. In the post-war period the trend in Old Testament scholarship and systematic theology was perceptibly in this direction. One has only to recall the work of G. von Rad in Old Testament theology. The fact remains that the decisive breakthrough in the interpretation of 'salvation as liberation' in the light of the Exodus was inspired by Ernst Bloch. In Bloch's atheistic interpretation of the Bible—indeed, in his 'philosophy of hope' as a whole—the Exodus plays a central role. The Exodus event, the liberation of slaves under Moses' leadership, is not only the foundation event in the Old Testament tradition but also at the same time the key to the 'permanent Exodus' programme, to a hope which is historical and social, and ultimately, to an 'Exodus from God' programme; it is the signpost indicating the road to a creative atheistic human life.

The use to which Bloch puts the Exodus theme is certainly open to criticism. His treatment of the biblical texts is very cavalier and sometimes quite arbitrary, as for example when he posits a popular revolutionary movement led by Moses as the historical basis of the saving Exodus event which the Bible clearly attributes to the initiative of Yahweh.

Or again, when he advances the thesis that a final atheistic phase is the logical outcome of the Exodus movement. And again when he plays down the importance of the creation motif in the overall pattern of the Exodus event. These and many other criticisms of Bloch's interpretation of the Exodus have been convincingly set out by many theologians, Old Testament scholars and systematic theologians alike. Yet credit must go to Bloch for having drawn attention to a central theme which had been largely neglected by the theologians. H. J. Kraus, for all his criticisms of Bloch's treatment of the Exodus, is right to insist: 'However critical we must be of any "expropriation" of a biblical concept, the fact remains that Bloch drew the attention of Christian theologians — who had made it exceptionally difficult for themselves by projecting a view of the total biblical witness in which the doctrine of the Messiah remained for the most part quite under-exposed — to a basic unifying element, to dynamically influential dimensions and motive forces which impelled the biblical witnesses to the eschatologically new and ultimate. Among these motivating forces, the Exodus has pride of place'.[71]

The 'theology of liberation' had good theological grounds for taking seriously this 'discovery' of an atheistic philosopher and for pursuing it resolutely, if critically and above all self-critically.

2. The problem to which the first of our two questions points certainly must be included in this critical self-critical reappraisal of the Exodus theme. The Old Testament attestation of the Exodus is extremely *diverse* and even very vague. Is it really possible to make such an event the basis for a theology (or even a politics) of liberation in the modern sense? This criticism deserves consideration.

The fact of the matter is that the Exodus event is presented in the Old Testament (and to some extent also in the New) as a salvation theme from a whole range of theological perspectives. In an essay on 'Salvation as Liberation in Israel', N. Lohfink, a Catholic Old Testament scholar, distinguishes at least three types of Exodus soteriology.[72]

(a) The soteriology of Deuteronomy and the Priestly document: *the Exodus as a once-and-for-all act.* We have already quoted the creed in which this soteriology is expressed (Deut. 26:5-9). Israel's salvation rests on a unique historical act of Yahweh, one which of course has its consequences in the history of salvation, namely, the 'fullness of life' in the Holy Land to which the Exodus gives access and which it has in view. The ancient creed ends with the words: 'He brought us to this place and gave us this land, a land flowing with milk and honey'. 'This land' — this is the present time of God's people made possible by the unique once-and-for-all saving act of Israel's God. The Exodus is 'an act of liberation'. 'But it is a contemporary reality in present blessings . . . . If for "Exodus" we substitute "the event of Christ", this does not greatly differ from the conception of many Christian theologians. The only difference is that in Deuteronomy everything is astonishingly concrete: here the blessing of salvation is dwelling in the land and enjoying its fruits unmolested by enemies'.[73]

(b) Another type of soteriology is found in the Yahwist tradition: *Curse and blessing in the history of the nations.* The Yahwist is, without question, the most original and individual of Old Testament theologians. The Exodus event does not have for him the unique key role it has in the Deuteronomic tradition. It is one of a series of saving events embracing in a universal sweep not only the salvation of Israel but that of all the nations. In this theology a dynamic factor of salvation history becomes visible. 'A movement is introduced into world history' from Abraham right down to the eschatological horizon by the promise and faithfulness of God. Lohfink thinks it should be possible 'to draw parallels' between this type of soteriology and 'modern theologies of salvation with a this worldly orientation'. But he warns us against trying to draw such parallels too directly and without the necessary qualifications. We must heed this warning. But Lohfink's categorical assertion that 'a theology of revolution can expect nothing from the Yahwist', I find much too unqualified and 'dogmatic'. In this direction, too, rigid alternatives have to be avoided in theology. The consistent Yahwist emphasis on God as the subject and agent of the transformation of the world in no way excludes the possibility of our being obliged as human beings to take the initiative in this transformation. While the Yahwist vision contains no explicit 'theology of revolution', this is not to say that a basis for revolutionary commitment cannot be sought and found in this tradition.

(c) The third type of Old Testament view of 'salvation as liberation' is that of _eschatological soteriology,_ as represented chiefly in the prophets of the Babylonian exile. Lohfink describes the new element here in terms which at first sight seem strangely anachronistic: 'Salvation as corrective to world structures?' 'Here we find statements about the transformation of fundamental structures . . . . In the book of Ezekiel, for example, we find a proposed future redistribution of the land of Israel in a strangely geometric way. In Deutero-Isaiah we find the old Davidic promises explicitly transferred to all Israel (Isa. 55:3-5). Does this mean there are to be no more kings in the coming salvation?

Something similar seems to occur in a certain stratum of Ezekiel 34, subsequently cancelled by glosses, where Yahweh removes his people's shepherds from office and makes himself the shepherd of his people. Finally, in Jeremiah 31:31-34 we find that very mysterious passage about the "new" covenant so very different from the old one: "I will set my law within them and write it on their hearts . . . . No longer need they teach one another to know the Lord; all of them, high and low alike, shall know me, says the Lord"'.[74]

Lohfink is certainly taking a risk when he seeks and finds in this context a connecting link with the contemporary 'theology of liberation', but *mutatis mutandis* he has some justification for doing so. There is the vision of a new society no longer subject to the structures now universally dominant. I take leave to doubt that this can be 'compared with just such utopian conditions as the "classless society"'. The prophetic vision concerns the structures of the coming kingdom of God and cannot be compared, therefore, to any utopia whatever, in the sense of a projection of conditions realizable here on earth. On the basis of this eschatological vision, however, he is right to seek a link with human efforts to transform the world: 'God's sovereignty as the end of every sort of human tyranny over human beings' is in fact an appropriate theme for the theology (and praxis) of liberation inspired by the Exodus.

The Old Testament witness to the Exodus theme is diverse and multidimensional. Is this any reason for calling it 'ambiguous'? Only, perhaps, if we use this term in a non-pejorative sense, meaning not that it is untrustworthy but rather, positively, that it is 'irridescent', that it has an illuminating diversity and force. It is irridescent because we cannot grasp or understand it directly since it shines out at a variety of levels and aspects of salvation and liberation. It is not the theme of Exodus itself which is relativized here but rather every view which would freeze it in some sectarian mold. If we understand the Exodus in this way, as event and as pattern, it remains an authentic element in every theology of liberation: the real legacy, the 'radical heritage' of the Old Testament for Christian soteriology.

The History of Jesus Christ as a History of Liberation

We now turn to the New Testament. Just as the Exodus event is the main centre of the prophetic message, so, too, the *events* associated with the name of *Jesus Christ* are the unique centre of the apostolic kerygma in a particularly concentrated way: the life, death and resurrection of Jesus of Nazareth. The question arises as to whether this New Testament centre is as important for our concern with freedom as the Old Testament centre is. I would answer that it is. The history of Christ is undoubtedly interpreted as eschatological liberation.

From the very beginning, even in the *message* of Jesus, it is expressly affirmed that the hour of freedom has struck. The text of Jesus' first sermon reads: 'The spirit of the Lord is upon me because he has anointed me; he has sent me to announce good news to the poor, to proclaim release for prisoners and recovery of sight for the blind; to let the broken victims go free, to proclaim the year of the Lord's favour'. This Isaiah passage is one of the classic statements of the Old Testament promise: the vision of the final 'Exodus' in which we find under the one rubric 'liberation' all the forms of human distress, the plight of the poor, the prisoners, the blind and the oppressed. The whole of Jesus' sermon (as Luke reports it) amounts to a pregnant and truly revolutionary claim: 'Today . . . . in your very hearing this text has come true' (Lk. 4:21). In other words, the eschatological promise is now coming to fulfilment. The hour of final liberation has struck for the poor and the oppressed, for the humbled and the excluded.

So Jesus' message. But it is at once matched by his *praxis,* too. And in his sufferings. Jesus lives and dies as deliverer, so to speak, as 'revolutionary of freedom'. To be sure, he is not a revolutionary in the sense that term was understood in his own day. He was not a Zealot; he did not champion the Jewish struggle for liberation from the Romans. But it was not because the Zealots were too radical for him that he marked his distance from them but rather because their idea of liberation was too shallow, too restricted, too narrowly confined within the context of political rebellion. The Exodus of freedom certainly has a political and economic dimension, of course; and this dimension is present also in Jesus' messianic entry into Jerusalem or when he overturns the tables of the moneychangers in the Temple. But the eschatological liberation has many facets, as does the human distress it promises to overcome. It has its spiritual and religious battlefront, reflected in the wide freedom Jesus exercised in refusing subservience to the law, in striking contrast to the pharisees. But it is also concerned with the material needs of the individual neighbour, as we see from the healings performed by Jesus. The liberation which Jesus' *praxis* is concerned to bring is an *all-round liberation.*

A significant pointer here is a 'formal'—in reality, however, a very substantial—aspect of Jesus' practice of freedom. I refer to his characteristic combination of a general and even universal openness towards all his fellow human beings irrespective of their cultural or social 'status' *with a definite partisanship for the poor and the disadvantaged.* Jesus was available for all, laying down no conditions qualifying his interest in and concern for the neighbour. He was there for poor and rich, for left-wingers and conservatives, for women and men. In those days, and even in our own, that was far from being a matter of course. Yet Jesus is no impartial, easy-going, colourless neutral; his words and his deeds display a commitment, a firm profile, a clear direction. Not for Jesus any vague amalgam of yes and no but always a frank yes and a frank no. He does not give his blessing to the traditional order. He promises and demands a definite transformation of human hearts and human orders—in favour of the weary and the heavyladen, the troubled and the oppressed.

Surprisingly enough, the response to this all-round praxis of freedom on Jesus' part was a strangely *all-round resistance.* We do well to remember that the rulers of two otherwise hostile powers—the Romans and the Jews—formed an unholy alliance precisely against Jesus and, insofar as we know of comparable cases, *only* against him. That was hardly accidental. Both sides of the 'establishment' of that time, both 'Church' and 'State' were in fact threatened by this freedom of Jesus. It was 'logical' that Jesus should be condemned to death by both sets of rulers. And so the New Testament 'revolution of freedom' was stifled by violence and death. In fact, however, the history of liberation in Jesus Christ, instead of coming to a premature end with his arrest, sufferings and death, found here its real meaning and its new beginning. It was not just as the history of his active life and ministry that the event of Jesus Christ became the basis and beginning of Christian freedom but also, and above all, as the Easter story, the fact of his cross and resurrection. The Christian 'revolution of freedom' revolves around these two central aspects of salvation — and liberation. To them we must now turn our attention.

The cross is undoubtedly the 'hard kernel' of the New Testament history of liberation. This is already apparent from the surprising amount of space and the theological importance assigned by the evangelists to the passion narratives. And the most pregnant formula for the apostolic Gospel is 'the Word of the Cross' (1 Cor. 1:18). The New Testament concept of redemption is inseparably connected with the cross: our 'release' (*apolutrosis*) took place in the sacrifice of Jesus Christ on Calvary, sealed 'through the shedding of his blood' (Eph. 1:7; 9:12 etc.).

Yet nowhere in the New Testament is there any suggestion that the cross of Christ was a tragic episode for which there are many historical parallels. It is there proclaimed as an incomparably unique event in which salvation is achieved. It reveals *eschatological* connections between sin and atonement, condemnation and reconciliation, judgement and redemption. In *this* sense, when what is really at stake is our ultimate human alienation and our final deliverance, Paul will 'think of nothing but Jesus Christ — Christ nailed to the cross' (1 Cor. 2:22). In the same way, the best illustration of the basic reference of the primitive Christian message of redemption and freedom is the gesture of John the Baptist as portrayed on the Isenheim altar by Matthias Grünewald: he points clearly and persistently to the figure of the crucified Lord.

The significance of this for the Christian view of freedom is that even experience of failure, suffering and death are taken up into the 'history of freedom'.

In his 'Stations on the Road to Freedom', Dietrich Bonhoeffer expresses this very clearly and movingly. This poem was written at a time when Bonhoeffer knew that in all probability his life would be brought to a violent end by his Nazi judges and hangmen. At this moment, looking back on his life, he understands it as, in spite of everything, 'stations on the way to freedom': the stations of 'discipline', 'action', but also of 'suffering' and 'death'. Not only the active life but the passive life, too, indeed, even life's end, is seen in the perspective of 'salvation as freedom'. The freedom experienced at the foot of the cross of Jesus is not gainsaid and erased even at the moment of frustration through the *passio humana et christiana*. In the present context, when we reflect on suffering and death as stations on the way to freedom, we shall do well to listen carefully to Bonhoeffer's testimony which, according to eyewitnesses, he bore out and maintained in his actual deportment right to his very last steps towards the place of execution.

Suffering

A change has come indeed. Your hands, so strong and active,
are bound; in helplessness now you see your action
is ended; you sigh in relief, your cause committing
to stronger hands; so now you may rest contented.
Only for one blissful moment could you draw near to touch
    freedom;
then, that it might be perfected in glory, you gave it to God.

Death

Come now, thou greatest of feasts on the journey to freedom
    eternal;
death, cast aside all the burdensome chains, and demolish
the walls of our temporal body, the walls of our souls that are
    blinded,
so that at last we may see that which here remains hidden.

Freedom, how long we have sought thee in discipline, action, and
  suffering;
dying, we now may behold thee revealed in the Lord.[75]

But it is not only the *oboedientia passiva* (suffering
obedience) of Christ which we are to see in the
Easter events, i.e. his atoning and redemptive
acceptance and sacrifice even unto death as the
basis of liberation, but, at the same time and
indissolubly connected with it, also his *oboedientia
activa* (active obedience) as pointer to our freedom.
The historical contours of the crucifixion of Christ
irrevocably fix the direction and content of a
'theology of liberation'. Only as a 'memorial of the
passion' (*memoria passionis*) is its authenticity
preserved. This formula was reintroduced into the
theological debate in recent years by J. B. Metz.
There is nothing really new about it — the *theologia
crucis* has always been influential in church history
as a very distinctive theological and spiritual option.
The relatively new emphasis given to this classical
tradition in more recent theology — justifiably so —
consists in the perception that this *memoria passionis*
is a 'dangerous idea'. What it means is following
Jesus in his solidarity with suffering humanity; i.e.
adopting that basic attitude expressed in the history
of Jesus not only at the end of his life but right from
the very beginning. To do so is *'dangerous'* because
devotion to those who suffer, in the spirit of Jesus,
means active identification with the oppressed and
the outcast — and this often leads to conflict with
oppressors and rulers. An authentic theology and
spirituality of the cross, far from encouraging an
uncritical glorification of human suffering, any
indulgent reconciliation with evil, on the contrary
challenges evil situations and conditions and is a
protest on God's behalf against the servitude
suffering imposes.

This aspect, this dynamic of the cross has often been muffled in the course of church history. The message of the cross has been mistaken by Christians and atheists for a consolatory ideology of false tolerance. Yet the theme itself was never completely obliterated. The Church continued to remember the sufferings of Jesus. We think for example of the Church's devotion to the sick and the weak, pursued with determination in spite of all forgetfulness. Christian *diaconia* in all its various forms but, above all, by its radical refusal to simply leave the defenceless to their fate and its basic acknowledgement that these defenceless ones have inalienable human rights when seen in the light of the cross of Christ, represents a unique contribution of the Church to human history. If this dimension of Christian faithfulness had been absent, the social dimensions of our culture and our history would have been very different.

Yet all too often these pioneering efforts have been too narrowly conceived. For the most part they have taken the form of charitable services, seldom really comprehensive in character, and only in very isolated instances have they been developed as *political programmes*. The typical church response to the social question right down to the present century has been the 'inner mission' pattern of service. I repeat, the positive aspects of this service are praiseworthy. Diaconia *really* is the classical battlefront of Christian love. What needs to be critically examined, however, is the notorious restriction of social service to this particular strategy. Ecumenical Christianity is gradually becoming aware of this today—with first attempts and the inevitable reactions. In this connection the World Council of Churches' Programme to Combat Racism could prove of vital importance. This Programme is in no sense a substitute for the philanthropic diaconal work of the universal Church. But it does draw attention, symbolically, to the necessary structural consequences of the *memoria passionis.* It reminds us that it is not enough to alleviate the consequences of evil, in this case the consequences of racism, by charitable works. We must also challenge the structural consequences of a racist spirit. The Programme to Combat Racism soon became the most criticized of all ecumenical programmes. Its questionable aspects and imbalances can and should be pointed out, of course. But the storms of criticism were surely due to a conscious or unconscious resistance to this radical venture on the part of the ecumenical movement. Even today panic seizes Christians whenever church groups venture out into the structural areas of political service.

Yet it is essential that this direction be taken today, soberly, self-critically, and without sectarianism. To understand and practice salvation as liberation we need not only a 'philanthropy of the oppressed' but also a 'pedagogy of the oppressed' (P. Freire) and, indeed, a 'politics of the oppressed'.

This brings me to the other essential aspect of the basic Christian history. In the apostolic preaching, the fact of Christ is presented not only as the life and death of Jesus of Nazareth but also, and indissolubly connected with it, the event of his *resurrection.* Only with the resurrection does the Gospel history acquire its utterly firm and immovable foundation. For many people in the Church, and certainly for our contemporaries outside it, the raising of Jesus from the dead, his resurrection, is a puzzling theme. Can we deny that 'resurrection' is indeed an esoteric motif? No wonder that some see it as a religious 'happening', something exclusively related to the 'beyond'; a useful symbol for transcendental meditation, perhaps, but hardly a realistic vantage point for any real form of liberation.

Such a view of resurrection is to my mind a misunderstanding. The New Testament message of the resurrection certainly has its mysterious aspects. Certainly it is related to the 'beyond', to the great question of death and *life after death*. None of this, thank God, can be eliminated from the biblical accounts. The question of death and of its power in human life is, after all, the basic question of human existence and will continue to be so. To a large extent it can be suppressed in our modern secularized culture. But this does not reduce its explosiveness as a question. A theology of liberation, in particular, would be foolish to forget this or to try to replace it with other emphases; by bursts of activism, for example. I say 'foolish' because to surrender the resurrection perspective would necessarily condemn Christian activity itself to a twilight of meaninglessness. Here too, Paul's words are relevant: 'If it is for this life only that Christ has given us hope, we of all men are most to be pitied' (1 Cor. 15:19). The resurrection hope has a quite specific application to this concrete threat overhanging every individual human being: the situation of our death.

But here again we must heed the principle: 'No false alternatives!' The eschatological mystery of resurrection is not a miracle outside history altogether. This event is presented by the New Testament witnesses in a decidedly *historical form*. It has a pre-history and a post-history. The former is the historical life of Jesus of Nazareth. The Risen One is no unhistorical and faceless spectre. He bears the unmistakable features of Jesus. In other words, in the resurrection this history, the message, deeds and sufferings of Jesus, do not dissolve into

140

metaphysics but are eschatologically validated. And the post-history of the resurrection is the confident venture of responding to this event, the praxis of resurrection in history.

As the disciples understood it, their Easter experience of Jesus was *the gift of the power to be free,* in a way otherwise quite unknown in their contemporary world with its obsession with coercive forces and its belief in fate. They understood it as a demonstration and promise that the power of fate, the power of death and all its gang of associates, was now broken for ever. These consequences of resurrection are stated by Paul in his immortal words: 'For I am convinced that there is nothing in death or life, in the realm of spirits or superhuman powers, in the world as it is or the world as it shall be, in the forces of the universe, in heights or depths —nothing in all creation that can separate us from the love of God in Christ Jesus our Lord' (Rom. 8:38f.).

The declaration of faith is followed by the response of action, namely, the astonishing *missionary* endeavour of the early Church. The apostles saw clearly that with such a message entrusted to them, they could not possibly let the world 'go hang'. In the light of their Easter experience, they saw the world and its history as a realm which had been 'invaded', opened up, and now basically open to them to enter—and they transformed it radically by their missionary activity. The departure to 'new frontiers' is possible. The principalities and powers still have power to oppress but they no longer have the last word. Humanity is no longer a slave but the child of *this* love. What is ventured on the basis of this hope is not a hazard, no desperate gamble. It is of a piece with this Easter prospect. That is the source and the goal of the life of faith.

141

One aspect here which I find quite remarkable about the 'resurrection praxis' of the apostles is the way it proceeds 'according to plan', so to speak, and is not just an expression of romantic enthusiasm. Certainly the apostles lived with a keen sense of the eschatological imminence of their coming Lord, but this in no way led them to withdraw from their historical context. They do not react blindly but consider carefully the most suitable ways of fulfilling their mission; they produce plans and develop a missionary strategy. We think of Paul and his carefully prepared *'campaign of hope'!*

With this venture into freedom, a new chapter begins in the history of human freedom. A real 'revolution of freedom' took place. Jürgen Moltmann is not indulging in romantic exaggeration when he states: 'The Christian faith is rightly understood as the beginning of a freedom hitherto unknown in the world'.[76] The historical significance of this becomes clear if we recall the *contemporary historical background.*

What ideas of human freedom were current in the late-Hellenistic world of apostolic times? Leaving aside the Stoic philosophy—the apostles seldom came into contact with its representatives—the intellectual climate was dominated by *gnosticism* so far as freedom (and salvation) were concerned. 'The gnostic attitude to life is dominated by a sense of alienation. Life means being away from home'.[77] The world is an unredeemed place and we are at the mercy of the powers and rulers of this estranged world. Not only is the body a prison but the soul, too, is the *'tabula rasa* of the demons'. Paradoxically enough, it was from this feeling that life is a condition of unlimited bondage that the gnostic 'concept of freedom' grew: everything is permitted. The world is so alien to us that we have no responsibility whatever towards it. Everything is therefore possible: extreme asceticism but also extreme libertinism. The gnostic practiced both with zeal. Both ways are a blind alley: freedom does not lie this way.

This was the world into which the Christian 'Exodus community' came. It listened to the gnostic message and understood it. The gnostics were right: the world is indeed in a sorry state. In the light of the cross of Jesus, that conclusion is wholly justified and to be taken quite seriously. And yet, that same cross cancels it out. The estrangement of the world is no longer an inexorable destiny. In the Easter event, all the tyrannical principalities and powers — even the last enemy, death — are dethroned. Humanity is no longer a slave in any valid sense. Freedom is now a possibility. 'For though everything belongs to you — Paul, Apollos, and Cephas, the world, life, and death, the present and the future, all of them belong to you — yet you belong to Christ, and Christ to God' (1 Cor. 3:22f.). The Exodus history arrives at its final goal. Salvation opens the way to freedom.

Christian Freedom: Its Dialectic and Its Praxis

Inspired by the biblical 'revolution of freedom', Christian theology — beginning with the apostle Paul — developed a new concept of freedom (as well as a new praxis of freedom). This new concept of freedom is characterized by an intricate dialectic. I want now to try to describe it in the particular context of 'salvation as liberation', but always keeping in view certain contemporary demands for freedom. This dialectic of freedom has three dimensions in particular which will be considered under the headings: controlled freedom; freedom in existence for others; freedom in hope.

1. *Controlled Freedom:* Seen from the Christian standpoint, freedom is controlled freedom. By 'controlled' I do not mean primarily 'controls' either from outside or from within us which threaten or limit our freedom. There are such limitations and we shall have to look at them, too. But from the Christian standpoint, freedom is controlled primarily in a wholly positive sense. It is *freedom in the covenant:* a freedom established for us and made accessible to us. It is highly significant that the covenant idea, the idea of the covenant between God and humanity, humanity and God, is proclaimed above all, in a highly concentrated form, in the context of precisely these two concrete liberation events—the Exodus in the Old Testament and the Easter event in the New. In other words, the Christian concept of freedom is understood in the quite concrete context of the covenant.

The significance of this context, firstly, so to say the *indicative* mood of freedom, the *promise* of freedom, is that human freedom is not a freedom without a foundation, without roots, dependent on itself. It is not something which has first to be wrested from the superior force of the world (as with the Stoics). We are not 'condemned to be free' (J. P. Sartre). For us freedom is a *permission* and a *possibility*—not by our achievement and effort, which always implies an element of strain and stress —because we are 'children of freedom', 'children of the promise' (cf. Gal. 4:28, 31) and enter into the inheritance secured for us. Paul is able to declare, therefore: 'Christ set us free, to be free men. Stand firm, then, and refuse to be tied to the yoke of slavery again' (Gal. 5:1).

But this quotation already points to the other aspect of 'controlled freedom': 'Stand firm . . . !' The freedom established within the framework of the covenant is also one which is wholly controlled by the biblical *imperative,* by an inherent *obligation.* It is not a freedom without responsibilities, therefore. The imperative 'Stand firm!' is not merely a rallying call, therefore, nor is biblical freedom a freedom controlled by laws. The Church has often promoted it in such terms and people outside the Church mostly understand it this way, even today. Christian ethics becomes a legalistic ethics. A Christian is someone who does certain things and refrains from doing certain other things. This is always a complete misunderstanding. For Jesus and the apostles the struggle against religious or moralistic legalism was one of the sharpest conflicts they had to engage in. Such legalism is a 'yoke of bondage'. 'Stand firm!' does not mean 'stick to your principles!', therefore, but *be true,* be faithful to the covenant; specifically, stand firm in the freedom made possible by the covenant and therefore always a faithful and never a faithless freedom. Freedom in faithfulness and faithfulness in freedom, this is the first emphasis in the dialectic of the Christian concept of freedom.

We find this dialectic in the Bible, above all, in the relationship between God and his people. The covenant of freedom and fidelity is the *leitmotif* of Israel's history (and of the Church's history, too). But at the same time it also applies to the relationship between human beings. It is significant that when the Bible speaks of the covenant of God with his people it uses a very intimate human language, employing for example the language of human sexual relationships in an amazingly frank way. God's fidelity is evidently intended to be understood in very concrete terms and, conversely, fidelity between human beings to be understood as a most profound and binding reality. Such fidelity is no mere empty convention but is rooted in and based upon the covenant.

Following the hint given by this reference to the language of the Bible, it may not be out of place to insert here a parenthesis on the contemporary practice of freedom in the realm of *sexual ethics*. Of course this is not the 'main front' in the battle for freedom in our world. Other more important ones will have to be mentioned before we conclude. But this is an important area of human responsibility and one which is also particularly connected with the problem of freedom, and concerns all of us. Moreover, there are people who claim that it is in area of sexuality (and perhaps only in this area?) that real progress has been made by humanity towards the achievement of freedom, in our days especially. There is nothing wrong, of course, with the removal of the taboo on sexual questions in recent years. Important aspects of human freedom are intimately connected with this. The discarding of legalistic and moralistic tendencies is wholly to be welcomed, especially in the light of the Bible and in view of the candour and freedom of the Old Testament affirmation of love between man and woman.

But this makes it all the more necessary to insist that candour and freedom here do not mean license. Real freedom between human beings is possible only by fidelity to the goal. Real liberation is experienced in voluntary fidelity, certainly not in an imposed fidelity which is subject to legalistic inspection. But in a *fidelity* which is voluntary; in the realistic recognition that freedom vis-à-vis the neighbour (as vis-à-vis God) means keeping faith and not in experimentation (even though this is what a genuine practice of freedom means in other areas). In this sense Christian freedom means 'controlled freedom'.

146

2. *Freedom in Existence for Others*

From the standpoint of Christian faith, freedom is the freedom of *love*. One is hesitant to use this word, so widely misused in the Church and in the world. Yet it is the fundamental word in the biblical message and intimately related to the Christian view of freedom. It is perhaps this which distinguishes this view of freedom most sharply from all others. Other ideas of freedom almost invariably presuppose and serve the interests of the (sovereign) Self; either defensively, as in classic Stoicism (I am free when I am alone with myself, autonomous and independent of the world and other people), or aggressively, as in German Idealism (the I posits the not-I), and this is made the model for freedom. In either case, the Self becomes the source of freedom.

The Christian view of freedom in no way denies the important aspects of freedom contained in the ideas just mentioned. My freedom does concern me and my independence of the world and other people. My freedom does concern my shaping of the non-Self, i.e. my action in shaping the environment. This is precisely what we have to affirm on the basis of the Exodus and in the light of the freedom of Jesus. What is roundly denied, however, is that this aspect of freedom, this reference to the self, is the be-all and end-all of freedom or even its heart and centre. From the standpoint of the Bible, the road to freedom does not begin with the Self, nor can it possibly end with the Self. Neither the Exodus nor the history of Jesus revolves around itself. Both are directed towards the neighbour, the others. Jesus' words indicate the direction: 'Whoever cares for his own safety is lost; but if a man will let himself be lost for my sake and for the Gospel, that man is safe' (Mk. 8:35). 'Christ achieves his freedom not by being self-controlled but rather by being with

147

others and for them'.[78] So long as I alone am free, I have not yet attained real freedom.

This is stated very clearly by Martin Luther in the two theses at the beginning of his *De libertate christiana:* 'A Christian is a free Lord over all things and subject to none. A Christian is a faithful servant of all things and subject to all'. The dialectical nature of evangelical freedom is finely captured in these two theses. It is freedom in relation to all things and all human beings. But it is the freedom of the lord who became a servant. It is not something we claim and achieve, possess as a privilege over against others. It means sensitivity to and consideration for the neighbour, for others; only as *co*-existence and *pro*-existence, existence *with* and existence *for* others, is it real freedom.

This view has implications for our contemporary praxis of freedom in the Church and in society. Take first the term *'coexistence'*. We are to see our own freedom as simultaneously and inseparably the freedom of others. In concrete terms: a Christian view of freedom can never be concerned merely with the freedom of Christians. I say this as a Christian who has been deeply marked by his experiences in Eastern Europe; in other words, as one who knows that religious freedom is neither trivial nor something to be taken for granted, but something we have to put ourselves on the line for. This is precisely why I want to stress that our life in a Marxist socialist society taught us—particularly in our efforts to democratize and humanize this society—that it is impossible to care for and strive for the freedom of Christians without at the same time caring for and striving for the freedom of other human beings, specifically, of atheist human beings. It was encouraging to see many Marxists coming to realize in the course of the Christian-Marxist dialogue that only as we strive for genuine freedom for others do we enjoy genuine freedom ourselves. This principle has to be remembered and put into practice — *mutatis mutandis* — in other situations, too. A freedom which in practice is all too ready to ride roughshod over the freedom of others is not real freedom. Freedom can only be maintained in a spirit of co-existence.

And it must also be maintained in a spirit of *pro-existence*. From the theological standpoint, freedom can only be understood not only as 'freedom *with* others' but ultimately only as 'freedom *for* others. How often this principle has been misunderstood! How frequently freedom has been claimed as the exclusive privilege and right of a person's own group, party or class, as the monopoly and trump-card of one group over against others! Think for example of the endless twistings and distortions of the word 'freedom' and its cognates in the polemics of the Cold War. People talked of the 'free world', the 'free society', the 'free press', 'free Europe', thinking not in terms of a calling against which the social conditions of a so-called 'free' society must be measured and judged but complacently and self-assuredly as something already possessed by its happy members, as an already proven virtue, indeed as an ace of trumps which could be slapped down triumphantly to beat all the rest!

Certainly western society has a vocation unique in history and still not utterly exhausted to achieve a system of freedom in which human rights are taken seriously. There is every reason to cherish and defend this system. In this respect, eastern society suffers from a depressingly long-standing backlog. We Christians in the East were keenly conscious of the bottlenecks and the restrictions on freedom in

Marxist socialist society. We were seriously concerned to achieve fuller freedom and struggled to do so. However, we knew that the complacent slogans of western 'freedom warriors' did not apply to us. People who regard freedom as something they possess and can boast about simply don't know what freedom really is.

I refer to this experience not in order to indulge in recriminations about the past but simply as something to be kept in mind when we reflect on our political existence today in the light of the Christian view of freedom. We are free in our societies only when our freedom takes the form of pro-existence in practice. This applies at the *national* level: real freedom only exists where the question of the access of the underprivileged to life and freedom is given serious consideration, i.e. only where freedom is understood and practiced not as an acquired privilege but as a social task and responsibility, namely, that of developing conditions and patterns of behaviour which promote solidarity and community.

It also applies at the *international* level. We are truly free in our respective nations — and particularly in Europe — only if we refuse to turn a blind eye to 'other people's' need for life and freedom; to disregard the needs of the people in Eastern Europe, for example, though no longer under the banner of the 'Cold War', of course, but appealing now (for example) to the slogan of *'détente'* and misinterpreting this to mean only a preoccupation with our own freedom from disturbance!

A further step is essential. Our practice of freedom in the Christian sense of the word includes being concerned not just for the interests of others in Europe (and in North America) but also for the interests of our fellow human beings in the 'Third

World' who are so vulnerable in the current international situation. One of the great services rendered by the ecumenical movement has been to make quite clear the essential ecumenical dimension of our social responsibility and so, too, of our understanding of freedom as concretely applied to the Third World. This may well prove to be the real test case for our freedom today—in the churches and in society.

In this setting, the challenge of ecumenical *'theologies of liberation'* will be most important for our theological existence today. These theologies are a conscious reflection of the situation of the poor in the 'Third' and 'Fourth' worlds (the latter being the term sometimes used for the poor sections of the population in all three worlds). The social 'context' of these theologies is very different from our own, therefore, and we cannot apply them directly to our own contexts. But this is not to say they are irrelevant to us. Quite the contrary. They are a challenge to our theory and practice of freedom. How do we exercise our freedom? By trying at all costs to maintain and if possible to extend our privileged positions? There are many symptoms suggesting that this is the automatic choice of the ordinary European consumer—not always with malice aforethought, of course, but often fairly unconsciously and resignedly.

We have here a major concrete challenge to theology, since such attitudes are proof of a dangerous shortsightedness, both politically and theologically. Sooner or later, the increasing gap between the economically rich and the economically poor will become quite intolerable and unmanage-able. A vigorous 'global world domestic policy' (C. F. von Weizsäcker) is a matter of life and death for us all. As for theology, what confronts us here in a very concrete form is the question of the well-springs of our freedom, the question of the theory and practice of freedom—and we are required to offer a committed answer. For real freedom is Christian freedom only if it is lived as freedom in existence for others.

3. *Freedom in Hope*

From the standpoint of Christian faith, freedom has a third aspect. Fashioned by the Exodus event and by the Christ event, freedom—Christian freedom— is experienced as freedom in hope. Two aspects of this keyword 'hope' must be kept together in our sights. *Firstly,* hope always includes the element of the *'not yet'.* In the first place, this means that the freedom of the Christian is not one long irresistibly triumphant march. It is a freedom under historical conditions, in life and in death, an imperilled freedom, a 'narrow' way constantly exposed to dangers from without and within, a freedom in conflict, so to say, a *libertas crucis,* a freedom of the cross. Strikingly enough, the central promises of freedom ring out against the background of human servitude at its deepest levels. We read, for example, in the eighth chapter of Romans, with reference to the whole of creation: 'Up to the present, we know, the whole created universe groans in all its parts as if in the pangs of childbirth' because of the 'shackles of mortality' (Rom. 8:21ff.). And, in the seventh chapter, where the reference is to the apostle's own life: 'But I perceive that there is in my bodily members a different law . . . . making me a prisoner under the law . . . . the law of sin' (Rom. 7:23). Unquestionably the human world is a deeply alienated world, objectively and subjectively. There is no 'good will' to tackle and solve the problem of freedom. Idealists and moralists who argue 'I can because I ought' are simply deceiving themselves. The real situation is quite different: 'The good which I want to do, I fail to do; but what I do is the wrong which is against my will . . . . Miserable creature that I am . . . . ' (Rom. 7:19, 24). There is no automatic triumph of freedom! Freedom comes only in hope.

Secondly, however, in the keyword 'hope' there is always another accent heard. Although the New Testament view of freedom bars the route of the idealists and moralists, it does not throw us into the opposite camp of the pessimists or so-called 'realists'. From Machiavelli down to the theoreticians of Fascism, there have never been lacking ideologies and systems which see through the illusions of the 'liberals' and take human servitude much more seriously. Yet these, too, turn their insight into a fetish. *Homo homini lupus* ('man is a wolf to his fellowmen')—this thesis is not simply a description of a good many political situations (one which has much evidence in its favour) but also an ideology and a practical method of dealing with the world. If you enter human society, be sure to take a whip or a bomb with you! What political human nature requires is not a strategy of freedom but a strategy of authority and a discipline as complete as you can make it!

This political philosophy and practice is quite incompatible with the Christian vision of the world. An indispensable and inseparable part of this vision is a hopeful outlook—indeed one in which the hope of freedom is central. We are not entitled to resolve the dialectic of the Pauline message of freedom, this time from the opposite end. The bondage of the creature is radical and universal. And yet, it is permitted 'in hope' (Rom. 8:21). Paul's groan— 'miserable that I am'—is radical and deep, yet it is

153

not his last word. It is immediately followed by the confident affirmation of deliverance, liberation, in 'God alone, through Jesus Christ our Lord!' and the shout of praise, 'Thanks be to God!' (Rom. 7:25). The human race is no *massa perditionis,* therefore, damned to all eternity. Even in its real bondage it already exists 'in hope' as a liberated race, a race to be liberated, or at any rate, a race which now can be liberated. It has indeed lost its magic, yet it has also been delivered from human bondage to an inescapable fate. There is hope of freedom.

This aspect of the Christian view of freedom can also provide guidance for our practice of freedom today and this in both of its dialectical emphases. It will be better to start with the *sobering* one. Under the conditions prevailing in our alienated world human freedom is always in practice an open road and never a condition of complete freedom. We in Europe and North America have often deceived ourselves on this score in our history of freedom and the struggle for freedom. Provisional and limited achievements of freedom — perfectly valid as such — have been magnified and transformed into 'salvation history'. In the process they have been distorted and corrupted. Many a movement for freedom has turned into a tyrannical establishment. The freedom fighter of yesterday or today, very often, conceals within himself the oppressor of tomorrow. Nearly half a century ago, in 1930, Ernst Bloch formulated this truth in these words: 'In the *citoyen* a *bourgeois* was concealed; heaven preserve us from what lies concealed in the comrade!' (The first thing a theologian should consider here, of course, is all that may lie concealed in the pious 'Christian man'!). This truth must not be used in a defeatist or cynical way. It is not to say that the commitment to freedom in the past was foolish or or that it is so today. But the positive meaning of this commitment is safeguarded by remaining free within it and towards it so that our vision may not be dulled by dogmatism and blinded to new possibilities of freedom but rather sharpened and clarified for seeing them. The 'eschatological proviso' of the Christian view of freedom is a still unexhausted and eminently helpful resource to this end.

Even more important and essential, perhaps, is the other aspect of the phrase, freedom in *hope*. I think it correct to say that the real threat to freedom in our world comes not so much from those who are idealistic about freedom but rather from the 'realists' who are weary of freedom or scornful of it. Certainly they hold a hand full of trumps. The chances of freedom in the nineteen eighties cannot be rated too high. The industrialized countries are threatened by a trend towards an increasingly organized, technologized, controlled and therefore manipulated society. The international scene is dominated by the super power-blocs who watch every change with suspicion and are only too ready to prohibit any 'irresponsible' freedom movement. In the developing countries, on the other hand, most people haven't enough to eat to be able to develop their freedom. In a world faced with such appalling problems, good wishes and ideals can accomplish little. Little wonder that a tendency to fatalism and superstition about power politics can be discerned in many places today.

What freedom demands of us is that, in spite of everything, we should resist such an attitude. Any real change, any progress in the direction of a more human world, is practically ruled out if we allow ourselves to be dominated by such an attitude. The biblical view of freedom provides the basis for the total rejection of fatalism. We must never forget that in view of the Exodus, in view of the history of our liberation in Jesus Christ, fate has been dethroned. No longer do the 'principalities and powers' (Rom. 8:38) hold the master key to our human world. They are still strong. We have to take the historical elements and the structures of political power seriously. But they are not omnipotent. It is possible for us and it makes sense to practice freedom — to seek in the spirit of Jesus to end oppressive personal and social conditions, to turn human hearts and social conditions in the direction of the promises of God's kingdom. This is really what corresponds to the real destiny of our world — 'in hope'. To know this and to act accordingly by standing firm in the liberty for which we have been set free — this is to live truly. Salvation, because it is both reconciliation and freedom, constrains us to serve the cause of peace and freedom in the world which Christ has redeemed.

Notes

1. The play on words in the original German is lost in translation. The emphasis on God as the 'Wholly Other' in the early Barth of the Commentary on Romans (*der Ganz-Anderer*) is linked here with the emphasis on God as the One who in Christ 'changes everything' (*der Ganz-Ändernder*), who makes all things new, which emerges in the later Barth of *Churchmatics* (e.g. *Church Dogmatics*, IV, 1 p. 316: 'the death and resurrection of Christ are *together* . . . . the basis of the *alteration* of the *situation* of the men of all times (Translator's note).

2. *Das Heil der Welt heute,* Preparatory German booklet for the Bangkok Missionary Conference on Salvation Today, 1973, p. 143.

3. *op. cit.* p. 143.

4. *Theological Dictionary of the New Testament,* ed. Kittel & Friedrich, tr. G. W. Bromiley, Eerdmans, Grand Rapids, Michigan 1970, vol. 7, p. 1002.

5. The text of Dr. Thomas's Bangkok speech is printed in the *International Review of Mission* (IRM), vol. LXII, No. 246, (April) 1973; here p. 159.

6. *op. cit.* p. 160.

7. *ibid.* p. 160f.

8. *ibid.* p. 161.

9. *ibid.* p. 199.

10. R. Bultmann, *Theology of the New Testament,* tr. K. Grobel, Charles Scribner's Sons, New York and SCM Press Ltd., London 1955, vol. 2, p. 155.

11. Kittel & Friedrich, *op. cit.* vol. 7, p. 973.

12. *ibid.* vol. 7, p. 976 (art. by Fohrer).

13. *ibid.* vol. 7, p. 978.

14. Bultmann, *op. cit.* vol. 2, p. 158f.

15. See C. E. B. Cranfield, *Epistle to the Romans,* Allenson, Naperville 1975, vol. 1, p. 404 and 419f.

16. Bultmann, *op. cit.* vol. 2, p. 157.

17. Cf. Oscar Cullmann, *The Christology of the New Testament,* tr. Guthrie & Hall, Westminster Press, Philadelphia 1959, p. 115ff.

18. Cullmann, *op. cit.* p. 115ff.

19. W. Grundmann, in Kittel & Friedrich, *op. cit.* vol. 9, p. 538f.

20. Novotny, *Biblicky Slovnik* I, p. 357.

21. Förster, in Kittel & Friedrich, *op. cit.* vol. 3, p. 288.

22. *ibid.* p. 289.

23. J. Schniewind, *Das Neue Testament Deutsch 2, Das Evangelium nach Matthäus,* 8th ed. Vandenhoeck & Ruprecht, Göttingen 1956, p. 14.

24. Otto Weber, *Grundlagen der Dogmatik* II, p. 195.
25. Weber, *op. cit.* p. 195.
26. W. Kasper, *Jesus der Christus*, Matthias-Grünewald-Verlag, Mainz 1974, p. 141.
27. Cf. W. A. Visser't Hooft, *The Kingship of Christ*, Harper, New York and London 1948. See also Jan M. Lochman, *Herrschaft Christi in der säkularisierten Welt* (Christ's Sovereignty in a Secularized World), 1967.
28. A. Ritschl, *Rechtfertigung und Versöhnung*, III. p. 383f.
29. E. Schweizer, *Jesus Christus, Herr über Kirche und Welt*, p. 178.
30. Luther, WA 10, 1, 1. p. 176.
31. *Religion in Geschichte und Gegenwart* (RGG), VI. col. 1378.
32. *ibid. ad. loc. cit.*
33. Otto Weber, *Grundlagen der Dogmatik* II, p. 203.
34. Barth, *Church Dogmatics* IV, 1. p. 273.
35. Büchsel, in Kittel & Friedrich, *op. cit.* xx vol. 1, p. 255.
36. *ibid.*
37. Bultmann, *Theology of the New Testament*, vol. I (ET. 1952), p. 285.
38. Weber, *op. cit.* vol. II, p. 214.
39. G. Greshake, in *Erlösung und Emanzipation*, p. 69f.
40. Emil Brunner, *The Christian Doctrine of Creation and Redemption* (Dogmatics II), tr. Olive Wyon, Westminster Press, Philadelphia and Lutterworth Press, London 1952, p. 283ff.
41. Greshake, *op. cit.* p. 70.
42. Gustaf Aulén, *Christus Victor:* An Historical Study of the Three Main Types of the Idea of Atonement, tr. A. G. Herbert, SPCK, London 1931. Paperback edition Macmillan Publishing Co., Inc., New York 1969 and SPCK 1970.
43. Aulén, *op. cit.* p. 84.
44. Cited by Aulén, *op. cit.* p. 36.
45. Cited by Aulén, *op. cit.* p. 97.
46. Weber, *op. cit.* vol. II, p. 238.
47. H. G. Pöhlmann, *Abriss der Dogmatik*, 2nd ed. p. 167.
48. Greshake, *op. cit.* p. 87.
49. Aulén, *op. cit.* p. 103ff.
50. Schleiermacher, *Glaubenslehre*, II, se. 108, 12.
51. Brunner, *op. cit.* p. 289.
52. Cf. Karl Marx, 'The philosophers have only *interpreted* the world differently; the point is, to *change* it' (*Essential Writings of Karl Marx*, ed. Caute, London 1967 and Macmillan Publishing Co., Inc., New York 1968, p. 43).
53. J. Müller, *Die Bergpredigt*, p. 124. See also my own study of the text in *'Die Not der Versöhnung'*.
54. J. Moltmann, 'Versöhnung in Freiheit' (Reconciliation in Freedom), in *Umkehr zur Zukunft*, p. 98.

55. The former President of the Federal German Republic. d. 1975.
56. H. J. Kraus, 'Erlösung im AT und NT' in RGG 3rd ed. II, col. 586.
57. Gutierrez, *A Theology of Liberation: History, Politics and Salvation*, tr. Inda & Eagleson, Orbis Books, Maryknoll, New York 1973, p. 6f. and p. 27.
58. *ibid.* p. 27.
59. W. Kasper, *op. cit.* p. 243.
60. G. Jacob, *Der Christ in der sozialistischen Gesellschaft*, p. 11.
61. Kasper, *op. cit.* p. 243.
62. Moltmann, *The Crucified God. The Cross of Christ as the Foundation and Criticism of Christian Theology*, tr. Wilson and Bowden. Harper & Row, New York and SCM Press Ltd., London 1974, p. 7.
63. *ibid.*
64. H. J. Kraus, *Grundriss systematischer Theologie. Reich Gottes: Reich der Freiheit*, p. 113.
65. H. Schlier, in Kittel & Friedrich, *op. cit.* vol. 2, p. 484ff.
66. Kraus, *op. cit.* p. 114.
67. See note 1.
68. See Arend Th. van Leeuwen, *Christianity in World History*, EHP 1964, p. 158ff.
69. Kraus, *op. cit.* p. 113.
70. Bonhoeffer, *Letters and Papers from Prison*, The Enlarged Edition ed. Bethge, Macmillan Publishing Co., Inc., New York and SCM Press Ltd., London 1972, p. 336.
71. H. J. Kraus, 'Das Thema "Exodus"' in *Essays in Biblical Theology* (in German only).
72. N. Lohfink, 'Heil als Befreiung in Israel', in *Erlösung und Emanzipation*, ed. L. Scheffczyk.
73. Lohfink, *op. cit.* p. 46.
74. Lohfink, *op. cit.* p. 49f.
75. Bonhoeffer, *Letters and Papers from Prison*, ed. Bethge, p. 371.
76. Moltmann, 'Die Revolution der Freiheit', in *Evang. Theologie*, 1967, p. 515.
77. On this, see K. Niederwimmer, *Der Begriff der Freiheit im NT*, p. 58ff.
78. H. Schlier, in Kittel & Friedrich, *op. cit.* vol. 2, p. 500.

first murder-over act of worship
murders in your heart